9

Essays and Studies 2002

Series Editor: Gordon Campbell
Associate Editor: Helen Lucas

The English Association

The objects of the English Association are to promote the knowledge and appreciation of the English language and its literature, and to foster good practice in its teaching and learning at all levels.

The association pursues these aims by creating opportunities of co-operation among all those interested in English; by furthering the recognition of English as essential in education; by discussing methods of English teaching; by holding lectures, conferences, and other meetings; by publishing journals, books, and leaflets; and by forming local branches.

Publications

The Year's Work in English Studies. An annual bibliography. Published by Oxford University Press.

The Year's Work in Critical and Cultural Theory. An annual bibliography. Published by Oxord University Press.

Essays and Studies. An annual volume of essays by various scholars assembled by the collector covering usually a wide range of subjects and authors from the medieval to the modern. Published by D. S. Brewer.

English. A journal of the Association, *English* is published three times a year by the Association.

The Use of English. A journal of the Association, *The Use of English* is published three times a year by the Association.

Newsletter. A *Newsletter* is published three times a year giving information about forthcoming publications, conferences, and other matters of interest.

Benefits of Membership

Institutional Membership

Full members receive copies of *The Year's Work in English Studies, Essays and Studies, English* (3 issues) and three *Newsletters.*

Ordinary Membership covers *English* (3 issues) and three *Newsletters.*

Schools Membership includes copies of each issue of *English* and *The Use of English,* one copy of *Essays and Studies,* three *Newsletters,* and preferential booking and rates for various conferences held by the Association.

Individual Membership

Individuals take out Basic Membership, which entitles them to buy all regular publications of the English Association at a discounted price, and attend Association gatherings.

For further details write to The Secretary, The English Association, The University of Leicester, University Road, Leicester, LE1 7RH.

Essays and Studies 2002

Writing Gender and Genre in Medieval Literature

Approaches to Old and Middle English Texts

Edited by
Elaine Treharne

for the English Association

D. S. BREWER

ESSAYS AND STUDIES 2002
IS VOLUME FIFTY-FIVE IN THE NEW SERIES
OF ESSAYS AND STUDIES COLLECTED ON BEHALF OF
THE ENGLISH ASSOCIATION
ISSN 0071–1357

First published 2002
D. S. Brewer, Cambridge

D. S. Brewer is an imprint of Boydell & Brewer Ltd
PO Box 9, Woodbridge, Suffolk IP12 3DF, UK
and of Boydell & Brewer Inc.
PO Box 41026, Rochester, NY 14604–4126, USA
website: www.boydell.co.uk

ISBN 0 85991 760 6

A catalogue record for this book is available
from the British Library

The Library of Congress has cataloged this serial publication:
Catalog card number 36–8431

This publication is printed on acid-free paper

Typeset by Joshua Associates Ltd, Oxford
Printed in Great Britain by
St Edmundsbury Press Ltd, Bury St Edmunds, Suffolk

Contents

Introduction

ELAINE TREHARNE AND GREG WALKER

IT WAS NOT SO very long ago that a book which advertised itself as
dealing with 'gender' would already have told potential readers not
only something about its contents but also a good deal about its
methodology and theoretical and ideological underpinnings too.
'Gender Studies' implied a certain range of feminist approaches, due
regard for a number of key thinkers and primary texts, and an
increasingly clear generic taxonomy of books either for, against, or
by women. Within little more than a single academic generation that
predictable critical landscape has been transformed beyond all recognition. 'Gender' as a field of academic concern has expanded and
developed to embrace a commonwealth of mutually informing disciplines, new approaches, new texts, and a whole new sex – men – have
been brought into the frame. 'Gender' as a term has been scrutinised,
nuanced, inverted, and teased into a field of play wide enough to
encompass interest in a variety of masculinities and feminisms, the
'straight', the 'queer', the bi-, trans- and a-sexual, the ancient, the
medieval, the early, late, and post-modern.

Medievalists, perhaps rather later onto the field than their modern-
ist colleagues, have nonetheless embraced the gendered as a distinct
and integral part of the writing and reading process (as distinct from a
subject of investigation) with no less enthusiasm, playing the field and
queering the pitch with studies that have explored, for example, the
range of masculinities on display in Chaucer's Canterbury pilgrimage,
or the gendered assumptions underlying religious writing for women
evident in texts such as the *Ancrene Wisse* and *Hali Meiðhad*.
Conferences on a range of related subjects have proliferated, and
new journals have been born reflecting the willingness of medievalists
of all kinds to embrace both new ways of reading and new things to
read.[1]

[1] Some recent publications in the field of Medieval Gender Studies include:
David Aers and Lynn Staley, *The Powers of the Holy: Religion, Politics, and
Gender in Late Medieval English Culture* (University Park, PA: University of
Pennsylvania Press, 1996); Karma Lochrie, Peggy McCracken, and James A.
Schultz, ed., *Constructing Medieval Sexuality* (Minneapolis, MN: University of
Minnesota Press, 1997); Louise Fradenburg and Carla Freccero, 3d., *Premodern*

The essays gathered in this volume provide both a summary sample of the current state of play – an indication of the range and scope of the ways in which an interest in or awareness of gender can transform conventional approaches to literary texts and genres – and an opportunity for a moment's reflection in the variety of possible roads ahead.

That gender is always already inflected by literary genre is, of course, not news. But the essays collected here provide useful examples of how the conventions behind and the expectations evoked by literary modes and genres help to shape what purports to be an entirely essential and/or socially constructed aspect of identity for the 'he', 'she', or 'I' of the literary text. Ranging across material from Old English Biblical poetry and hagiography to the late Middle English romances and fabliaux, the essays are united by a commitment to a variety of traditional scholarly methodologies. But each examines afresh an important aspect of what it means to be man or woman, husband, son, mother, daughter, wife, devotee or lover in the context of a particular kind of medieval literary text.

Hugh Magennis examines the representation of a woman who seems to confound the gender expectations of the genre which she inhabits and which has called her forth. Judith, the biblical slayer of Holofernes, eponymous protagonist of one of the most powerful and evocative of Old English narrative poems, must transcend the wise-speaking, peace-weaving, hall-gracing qualities that are traditionally the lot of women in heroic poetry, and slaughter Holofernes in his sleep. Magennis sensitively shows how the *Judith*-Poet negotiates the potential stigma that would naturally attach itself to such obvious markers of 'monstrosity' as are evident in the biblical Judith (sexual manipulativeness and murderous violence) while allowing his protagonist to remain something more than merely an 'honorary man'. A similar interest guides David Salter's essay, in which two further female protagonists in a predominantly male-oriented heroic genre are the subject of interest:

Sexualities (London: Routledge, 1996); Allen J. Frantzen, *Before the Closet: Same-Sex Love from Beowulf to Angels in America* (Chicago: University of Chicago Press, 2000); Britton J. Harwood and Gillian R. Overing, ed., *Class and Gender in Early English Literature: Intersections* (Bloomington and Indianapolis, IN: Indiana University Press, 1994); Ruth Evans and Lesley Johnson, ed., *Feminist Readings in Middle English Literature: The Wife of Bath and All Her Sect* (London: Routledge, 1994); Clare A. Lees, ed., *Medieval Masculinities: Regarding Men in the Middle Ages* (Minneapolis, MN: University of Minnesota Press, 1994).

the anonymous Empress in the fourteenth-century Middle English romance *Octavian*, and Olympias, the mother of the chief protagonist in *King Alisaunder*. Here Salter deliberately chooses his heroines for the contrasts that they offer: the former being a highly conventional, self-effacing and virtuous wife and mother in the approved romance fashion, the latter a far more troublesome and idiosyncratic figure. In each case, however, Salter reveals affinities as well as dissimilarities of treatment in the two texts, as distinct generically inflected narrative modes – first the hagiographic and potentially tragic, then the comic – dominate the narrative and determine the representation of the suffering females portrayed.

Comedy is also at the heart of Greg Walker's essay, which revisits that most problematic of fabliau males, Absolon in Chaucer's *Miller's Tale*. Looking afresh at the range of critical approaches to the parish clerk's transgressive 'misdirected kiss', Walker offers a new reading of the incident that draws out the implications of both Absolon's conception of his own masculinity and his painful misreading of Alisoun's womanhood. Also focused on Chaucer is Elaine Treharne's study of the Wife of Bath, which draws upon sociolinguistic theory and practice to revisit the oft-traversed field of the Wife's 'feminism' and power. Drawing upon some seminal sociolinguistic conclusions concerning the nature and value of 'women's speech', Treharne offers a trenchant rebuttal of those readings that have seen Chaucer as assaying a new and liberating approach to female utterance in the Wife's *Prologue*.

The essays by Anne Marie D'Arcy and Mary Swan examine religious writing about – and in one case ostensibly by – women, *The Prioress's Tale* and accounts of the life and miracles of St Veronica respectively. The subject of Mary Swan's essay is St Veronica, a saint who was thought to be virtually unknown in Anglo-Saxon England, and exists in cultural memory primarily through a series of fragmentary allusions and narrative vignettes that were gradually merged into a single, episodic narrative. Swan's careful comparative study of the surviving manuscripts containing versions of the Veronica story or allusions to her name suggests that interest in her life might have been earlier and more regional (the associations with Exeter seem compelling) than has hitherto been thought. Moreover that interest may well, as Swan argues, give cause to wonder whether that essentially 'feminine' form of affective piety with which Veronica is associated may also have enjoyed a longer history in these islands than most accounts suggest.

D'Arcy offers a wide-ranging analysis of *The Prioress's Tale*, focusing on the Anti-Semitism of the *Tale*, and on the theological complexities and historical resonances integral to the narrative. In her detailed consideration, D'Arcy evaluates the positioning of the narrator, and Prioress's own understanding of the Marian legend. Issues of literacy, myth, and critical response to this troubling *Tale* inform the discussion and challenge conventional wisdom on the *raison d'être* of this work.

This volume thus brings together a range of approaches to a selection of important medieval genres. The inclusion of Old and Middle English literature, with the focus on Chaucer's *Canterbury Tales* among the latter, also assists in dissipating boundaries of periodicity, demonstrating continuities in the writing of gender in the Middle Ages. The approaches are valid for all texts in which the issue of gender is uppermost in critical evaluation: Hugh Magennis suggests ways forward for a closer analysis of vocabulary pertaining to physical appearance and the appropriation of typically male heroic actions; Mary Swan demonstrates that there is still much work to be done not only in the assessment of saints' cults and the manuscript transmission of *vitae*, but also in appraising the potential readership of this most prolific of medieval genres. David Salter illustrates through his discussion the ways in which 'invisible' women – essential prerequisites to driving the plot in Romance – can be closely examined for the variety of roles and depictions within this genre. Within the Chaucer texts under analysis here, Walker, Treharne and D'Arcy evince three very different methodologies, but the new readings offered on fabliau, secular monologue, and religious verse, while consolidating and enhancing previous scholarship, also show the interpretative flexibility of this magisterial author. The debate on reading Chaucer continues, as it does for all the texts included here, and the flourishing field of gender studies, and it is to this debate that these essays contribute.

Gender and Heroism in the Old English Judith

HUGH MAGENNIS

THE PROTAGONIST OF THE Old Testament poem *Judith*[1] is one of the most powerful and active female figures in Old English literature, and one of the most 'heroic' in her actions. The Old English poem is an imaginative adaptation of the Book of Judith, but one which in its surviving form treats only the climax of the biblical narrative (corresponding to Judith 12. 10 onwards), where Judith is particularly in the foreground. It describes how, having gained access to the camp of the Assyrians who are besieging her people in their city of Bethulia, Judith enters alone the tent of the leader Holofernes and beheads him there, clear-sightedly taking advantage of his lust and drunkenness to draw him to his death. In killing Holofernes in his tent, Judith, like Beowulf against Grendel's mother and later against the dragon, performs the archetypal heroic act of venturing alone into the lair of the monster and there destroying it. Her deed leads to triumph over the powerful enemy which has been oppressing her people.

But within the ideological world of traditional Old English poetry heroic action is the prerogative of men, not women. Women have an honoured role in the heroic world, as reflected in poems such as *Beowulf*, *Widsith* and *Waldere*, but that role does not normally include engaging in violent action. Women exercise agency in ways other than carrying out heroic acts. In situations of danger or crisis, they make their contribution not through physical action but through words, of wisdom, incitement and advice. And they are often portrayed passively, as in the representation that Joyce Hill has characterised as that of the *geomoru ides*.[2] A key role that some women play is that of 'peace-weaver', a role that allows them to exercise decisive power, although it could also be said that peace-weavers are really always pawns in a

[1] *Judith*, ed. Mark Griffith (Exeter: University of Exeter Press, 1997).
[2] Joyce Hill, '"þæt wæs geomuru ides!" A Female Stereotype Examined', in *New Readings on Women in Old English Literature*, ed. Helen Damico and Alexandra Hennessey Olsen (Bloomington and Indianapolis, IN: Indiana University Press, 1990), pp. 235–47.

larger game, 'moved' by their elders and the patriarchal tribal leadership.[3]

The traditional gender-role demarcation of heroic society is notably expressed in a passage on the complementary roles of the ideal lord and lady, in the gnomic poem *Maxims I*:[4]

> Bu sceolon ærest
> geofum god wesan.   Guð sceal in eorle,
> wig geweaxan,   ond wif geþeon
> leof mid hyre   leodum, leohtmod wesan,
> rune healdan,   rumheort beon
> mearum ond maþmum,   meodorædenne
> for gesiðmægen   symle æghwær
> eodor æþelinga   ærest gegretan,
> forman fulle   to frean hond
> ricene geræcan,   ond him ræd witan
> boldagendum   bæm ætsomne.   (lines 82–92)

[Both must above all be generous in gifts. Battle and war must flourish in the man, and the woman must thrive beloved among her people. She must be of bright manner and keep counsel, and she must be liberal with horses and treasures; in counsel over the mead among the band of warriors she must always and everywhere greet the leader of the noblemen first, immediately present the cup to her lord's hand; and she must understand what is wise for both of them together as possessors of the hall.]

In this passage the lord and lady act in concert as 'possessors of the hall' in a shared social purpose. The lord is associated with battle and the lady with courtly manners and with qualities of discretion and wisdom (*rune healdan, ræd witan*).

---

[3] See Hill, '"þæt wæs geomoru ides!"', and L. John Sklute, '*Freoðowebbe* in Old English Poetry', *Neuphilologische Mitteilungen* 71 (1970), reprinted in *New Readings on Women*, ed. Damico and Olsen, pp. 204–10; see also Richard J. Schrader, *God's Handiwork: Images of Women in Early Germanic Literature*, Contributions in Women's Studies 41 (Westport, CT: Greenwood, 1983); Jane Chance, *Woman as Hero in Old English Literature* (Syracuse, IL: Syracuse University Press, 1986); and Gillian R. Overing, *Language, Sign, and Gender in Beowulf* (Carbondale, IL: Southern Illinois University Press, 1990), pp. 68–107.

[4] Citations of and references to Old English poems other than *Judith* follow *The Anglo-Saxon Poetic Records*, ed. George Phillip Krapp and Elliott Van Kirk Dobbie, 6 vols (New York, 1931–53).

Female virtue is highly valued in the Old English heroic tradition, and anxious disapproval is expressed towards those women whose behaviour is contrary to its principles, like the threatening (Mod)Thryth in *Beowulf* (lines 1931–62), who resists the gaze of the warriors and is associated with violence, and like the 'fyrwetgeornra', 'more daring', women in *Maxims I* (line 101) who are unfaithful to their husbands. Female virtue is epitomised in the tradition in the dutiful and courteous figures of Wealhtheow, Freawaru, Hildeburh and Hygd in *Beowulf*. These noble women are modest and wise and their actions are guided by their identification with the communal good of their patriarchal society. They are supportive of men and also dependent on men. Such women are not normally expected to possess physical courage or prowess. As R. E. Kaske points out, courage and prowess, when required by the circumstances in which a woman finds herself, are seen as 'to be somehow obtained or enlisted from elsewhere'.[5] Wealhtheow, for example, as Kaske notes, is 'a woman of graciousness, tact, and insight, justifiably concerned about a violent future which she foresees but can do nothing to prevent ([*Beowulf*, lines] 1168–87); her only recourse is a covert appeal to the strength of Beowulf and the Geats ([lines] 1215–31)'.[6]

Only when the normal possibilities for heroic action have been removed or shown to be ineffectual and help cannot be 'obtained or enlisted from elsewhere' (to use Kaske's phrase again) do females engage in violence, and even then only rarely and problematically, as happens in the case of Grendel's mother avenging her son in *Beowulf*. We might also think of the story of Guðrún in the Old Norse heroic tradition, a tradition closely related to that of Old English. Guðrún enthusiastically exercises savage vengeance against her husband when her brothers have been killed.[7] Grendel's mother and Guðrún present highly disturbing instances of female behaviour, however, and neither of them would have been regarded from within the heroic perspective as an image of admirable femininity. Grendel's mother represents the forces of darkness rather than virtue, and the vengeance of Guðrún becomes a monstrous travesty of both heroic

---

[5] R. E. Kaske, '*Sapientia et Fortitudo* in the Old English *Judith*', in *The Wisdom of Poetry*, ed. Larry D. Benson and Siegfried Wenzel (Kalamazoo, MI: Medieval Institute Publications, Western Michigan University, 1982), pp. 13–29 and 264–8 (at p. 15).

[6] Kaske, '*Sapientia et Fortitudo*', pp. 15–16.

[7] *Atlakviða*, ed. and trans. Ursula Dronke, *The Poetic Edda*, 2 vols (Oxford: Clarendon Press, 1969–97), I (*Heroic Poems*), pp. 1–12.

and maternal values, for it includes deliberately killing her own children.

In a literature, therefore, which normally assigns to females (as to males) circumscribed gender-specific roles, the Judith of the Old English poem immediately stands out as an exception to the norm. Here is a female who does engage in violence and who takes upon herself a terrifying heroic task.[8] She also takes over the role of leader of her people, ordering the warriors (*bebead*, line 144, *het*, line 171) and making a commander's speech of encouragement before battle, like Hnæf in *The Battle of Finnsburh* (lines 10–12) or Byrhtnoth in *The Battle of Maldon* (lines 17–21). Judith exhorts,

> Beraỗ linde forỗ,
> bord for breostum   ond byrnhomas,
> scire helmas   in sceaỗena gemong,
> fyllan folctogan   fagum sweordum,
> fæge frumgaras.   (lines 191–5)

[Bear your shields forth, your bucklers before your breasts, and your mailcoats, your shining helmets in the midst of your enemies; cut down the leaders with your gleaming swords, the doomed chieftains.]

Among the heroic epithets applied to Judith are *ellenrof* (lines 109 and 146), 'valorous', *collenferhỗ* (line 134), 'brave-hearted', and *modig* (line 334), 'courageous', all of which are also used of the male hero Beowulf (*Beowulf*, lines 340, 1806 and 1812, respectively). As Patricia Belanoff points out, Judith also resembles Beowulf in possessing *blæd*, 'glory' (*Judith*, line 122; *Beowulf*, line 1761), and both heroes are *æỗele*, 'noble' (*Judith*, lines 176 and 256; *Beowulf*, line 198).[9]

The men of the city of Bethulia have been unable to challenge

---

[8] As Michael Swanton comments, 'It is not the act itself which causes disquiet . . . but the fact that it is undertaken by a woman', *English Poetry before Chaucer* (Exeter: Exeter University Press, 2002), pp. 166–78 (at p. 174); see also Swanton's essay 'Die altenglische Judith: Weiblicher Held oder frauliche Heldin', in *Heldensage und Heldendichtung im Germanischen*, ed. Heinrich Beck, Ergänzungsbände zum Reallexicon der Germanischen Altertumskunde 2 (Berlin and New York: Walter de Gruyter, 1988), pp. 289–304.

[9] Patricia A. Belanoff, '*Judith*: Sacred and Secular Heroine', in *Heroic Poetry in the Anglo-Saxon Period: Studies in Honor of Jess B. Bessinger, Jr.*, ed. Helen Damico and John Leyerle (Kalamazoo, MI: Medieval Institute Publications, Western Michigan University, 1993), pp. 247–64 (at p. 253).

Holofernes and his army and despondently (*geomormodum*, line 144) they await the outcome of Judith's expedition. Similarly, the Danish warriors in *Beowulf* were unable to challenge Grendel and they gloomily awaited the result of the male hero Beowulf's fight with Grendel's mother, wishing but not expecting – *wiston and ne wendon* (*Beowulf*, line 1604) – to see their leader again. In killing Holofernes and inspiring her people, Judith takes on the role of the male hero of traditional poetry. She has had to do so because in the Bethulia of *Judith* the normal possibilities for heroic action are not available or have been deemed ineffectual in dealing with the Assyrian threat. Something different is needed to overcome this threat.

The Old English poet strives to present that 'something different' in such a way that Judith may take on the heroic role without losing her femaleness, without becoming either monstrous or some kind of honorary male. The very fact of male-directed female violence at the heart of the story has been discerned in recent criticism as a source of anxiety in the poem,[10] resisting assimilation to traditional categories, but it is one that the poet has worked to address both in the characterisation of the unspeakable Holofernes, a figure of evil who is portrayed as deserving all he gets, and in the treatment of the potentially transgressive Judith. The element of sexual allure and manipulativeness on the part of Judith is firmly edited out in the Old English poet's adaptation of the biblical Book,[11] but her female qualities remain very evident in the poem. Indeed the editing-out of the sexual allure and manipulativeness (one kind of feminine stereotype) has the effect of rewriting Judith as in key respects an unthreatening model of female virtue. Holofernes's downfall is caused by his own lust and drunkenness rather than by any disconcerting

---

[10] Karma Lochrie writes that Judith 'disables masculine identity' and 'is a threat to the masculine heroic order she exploits': 'Gender, Sexual Violence, and the Politics of War in the Old English *Judith*', in *Class and Gender in Early English Literature: Intersections*, ed. Britton J. Harwood and Gillian R. Overing (Bloomington and Indianapolis, IN: Indiana University Press, 1994), pp. 1–20 (at p. 10). See also Alexandra Hennessey Olsen, 'Inversion and Political Purpose in the Old English *Judith*', *English Studies* 63 (1982), 289–93; John P. Hermann, *Allegories of War: Language and Violence in Old English Poetry* (Ann Arbor, MI: University of Michigan Press, 1989), pp. 173–98; Susan Kim, 'Bloody Signs: Circumcision and Pregnancy in the Old English *Judith*', *Exemplaria* 11 (1999), 285–307.

[11] See my article, '"No Sex Please, We're Anglo-Saxons"? Attitudes to Sexuality in Old English Prose and Poetry', *Leeds Studies in English*, New Series 26 (1995), 1–27 (at pp. 12–13).

seductiveness on the part of Judith. Her qualities of radiance and wisdom, along with her courage, are what are most emphasised in her portrayal in the poem.[12]

The poet had the opportunity to suggest that in killing Holofernes Judith transcended female weakness and acted 'manfully'. Women acting 'manfully' was a theme not unfamiliar in early medieval literature,[13] and the Book of Judith itself makes use of this idea with reference to Judith, when the people praise her because she has acted 'manfully' – as the Vulgate puts it, 'quia tu fecisti viriliter' (15. 10). This reference is omitted in the Old English version's free adaptation of the biblical passage in question, as indeed is the accompanying reference to the people's glorification of Judith's chastity – 'eo quod castitatem amaveris' ['because you loved chastity'].

It has been argued that the image of the heroic woman in the poem should be understood primarily in terms of a different traditional model of female virtue, that of the virgin martyr of hagiography.[14] In my view, there is some influence from hagiography apparent in the treatment of Judith but she is essentially a Germanic noblewoman rather than a Christian virgin martyr. Hagiographical features of *Judith* include its strongly oppositional treatment of narrative, recalling the good versus evil structural pattern of the *passio* (in the biblical original Holofernes is a much less fierce opponent); also, like a saint, Judith prays to the Lord and to the Trinity for grace and victory and she herself shows true faith in her strife against an evil enemy; she is referred to with saintly epithets, *halig* (lines 56, 98, 160 and 260) and *eadig* (line 35); and, though she is not martyred, she even receives a kind of symbolic equivalent of the heavenly prize of the saint at the end of the narrative when her people glorify her and she is given the reward of the spoils of Holofernes.

On the other hand, Judith is not actually a martyr, and does not

---

[12] On the wisdom of Judith, see Kaske, 'Sapientia et Fortitudo', and Margaret Locherbie-Cameron, 'Wisdom as a Key to Heroism in *Judith*', *Poetica* 27 (1988), 70–5.

[13] See Gopa Roy, 'A Virgin Acts Manfully: Ælfric's *Life of St Eugenia* and the Latin Version', *Leeds Studies in English*, New Series 23 (1992), 1–27.

[14] See, for example, Rosemary Woolf, 'Saints' Lives', in *Continuations and Beginnings: Studies in Old English Literature*, ed. E. G. Stanley (London: Thomas Nelson and Sons, 1966), pp. 37–66 (at p. 64); James F. Doubleday, 'The Principle of Contrast in *Judith*', *Neuphilologische Mitteilungen* 72 (1971), 436–41 (at p. 438); Belanoff, '*Judith*: Sacred and Secular Heroine', pp. 256–7; Griffith, *Judith*, pp. 80–2; Patrick W. Conner, 'Religious Poetry', in *A Companion to Anglo-Saxon Literature*, ed. Phillip Pulsiano and Elaine Treharne (Oxford: Blackwell, 2001), pp. 251–67 (at p. 261).

really go to heaven at the end of the poem. And the hagiography-like preoccupation with her virginity and her chastity, which some critics have highlighted in their analysis of the poem,[15] is not apparent on close examination. The inherited story of Judith is of a widow who has the experience and knowledge to overcome Holofernes in his tent, and I think that in the Old English poem the heroine can be seen more convincingly as a widowed Germanic noblewoman than a youthful virgin martyr. The existing text of the poem has nothing inconsistent with the idea of Judith as a widow and certainly we are not obviously encouraged to see her as a virgin. As Kathleen Parker has recently pointed out, of the terms connoting 'female' that are applied to Judith in the poem – *ides* (lines 14, 55, 58, 109, 128, 133, 143 and 340), *mægð* (lines 35, 43, 78, 125, 135, 145, 254, 260 and 334), *meowle* (lines 56 and 261) and *wif* (line 148) – '[a]ll are used at some point in the corpus to refer to females who have been sexually active'.[16] Parker refers perceptively to 'the restraint shown by the poet in his choice of terms to refer to Judith as chaste' and to the 'de-emphasiz[ing of] the role her chastity plays in the text'.[17] The chastity of the heroine is a concern for Ælfric in his Old English paraphrase of the Book of Judith[18] but does not receive attention in the poem, which would not be the case in a typical life of a virgin martyr. As noted above, the poet leaves out the reference to the people's praise for Judith's chastity at the end of the story. Female chastity was evidently highly valued in early Germanic society,[19] and we have no reason in the poem to doubt that the virtuous woman Judith is chaste, but the aspect of chastity is not one highlighted by the poet's treatment.

In the Book of Judith, of course, Judith is not a noblewoman but a respected townswoman, but in the Old English poet's recreation of the story in Germanic terms this widow is fitted into the aristocratic social structure of the heroic world, meriting the epithets *beagum gehlæste* (line 36) ['laden with bracelets'], *hringum gehrodene* (line 37) ['adorned

---

[15] See, for example, Ian Pringle, ' "Judith": The Homily and the Poem', *Traditio* 31 (1975), 83–97 (at p. 96); Chance, *Woman as Hero*, pp. 31–52.

[16] Kathleen Parker, 'Is the Old English *Judith* Beautiful?', *Annali Instituto Universitario Orientale, Napoli, Sezione Germanica*, New Series 2 (1992), 61–77 (at p. 75).

[17] Parker, 'Is the Old English *Judith* Beautiful?', pp. 75–6.

[18] Ed. Bruno Assmann, *Angelsächsische Homilien und Heiligenleben*, Bibliothek der angelsächsischen Prosa 3 (Kassel: G. H. Wigland, 1889; reprinted with a supplementary introduction by Peter Clemoes, Darmstadt: Wissenschaftliche Buchgesellschaft, 1964), pp. 102–16.

[19] See Chance, *Woman as Hero*, pp. 7–9.

with rings'], *beahhrodene* (line 138) ['adorned with bracelets'] and *golde gefrætewod* (line 171), ['adorned with gold']. These epithets recall the similar terms used of noblewomen elsewhere in Old English verse.[20] As Peter Lucas has pointed out, aspects of Judith's portrayal also conform to the classic observations about Germanic women made by the Roman historian Tacitus.[21]

Also consistent with Judith's presentation as a Germanic lady is the poem's lack of emphasis on her physical beauty and sexual attractiveness. This lack of emphasis should not be seen, however, as has been claimed, as 'de-centering' Judith's femaleness.[22] It is notable that images of women in surviving Old English heroic poetry concentrate on mental qualities and on their external adornment, but do not normally specify physical beauty and do not highlight sexual attractiveness. This observation can be illustrated by quoting from the passage in which Wealhtheow is first introduced in *Beowulf*:

> Eode Wealhþeow forð,
> cwen Hroðgares,   cynna gemyndig,
> grette goldhroden,   guman on healle,
> ond þa freolic   wif ful gesealde
> ærest Eastdena   eþelwearde . . .
> sincfato sealde,   oþþæt sæl alamp
> þæt hio Biowulfe,   beaghroden cwen
> mode geþungen,   medoful ætbær;
> grette Geata leod,   gode þancode
> wisfæst wordum.   (lines 612–16 and 622–6)

[Wealhtheow came forth, Hrothgar's queen, mindful of etiquette. Adorned with gold she greeted the men in the hall and that noble woman gave the cup first to the guardian of the homeland of the East Danes . . . She offered the precious cup until the time arrived when the ring-adorned queen, distinguished in mind, carried the mead-cup to Beowulf. She greeted the chief of the Geats and, wise in words, gave thanks to God.]

---

[20] See Parker, 'Is the Old English *Judith* Beautiful?', pp. 68–9.
[21] Peter J. Lucas, '*Judith* and the Woman Hero', *Yearbook of English Studies* 22 (1992), 17–27 (at 25–6). Lucas's reading of Judith is in key respects similar to mine, but he sees Judith's role in the poem as grow[ing] out of a conformity with ideal female behaviour in a heroic society (p. 17), whereas I am arguing here that her role is dauntingly at odds with the female behaviour appropriate to her place in society.
[22] Belanoff, '*Judith*: Sacred and Secular Heroine', p. 252.

The passage begins by defining Wealhtheow in terms of her relation-ship to Hrothgar, and then speaks of her courtesy and the impressive jewellery she wears, before going on to refer to the quality of her mind and her wisdom in speech. It does not mention her looks or figure. One might argue that in a sense all the features of Wealhtheow highlighted in the poem are aspects of her beauty (as implied by the approach to beauty taken by P. B. Taylor in a recent essay),[23] but if so this beauty is the beauty which emanates from her whole person, not the beauty of her physical qualities, and it is not presented in terms of sexual attractiveness. As Michael Swanton has noted,[24] there is a 'largely asexual quality' to much Old English verse, to which the lack of poetic interest in female beauty may be seen to contribute. Nothing was mentioned about beauty in the description of the ideal noble lady in *Maxims I* (as quoted above), though the necessity of courtly manners and wisdom was specified. Interestingly, the only woman in *Beowulf* who seems to be described as beautiful is the 'questionable' character (Mod)Thryth, to whom the epithet *ænlicu* (line 1941), 'peerless, unique', is applied. Here *ænlicu* is likely to refer to appearance, since (Mod)Thryth is presented as far from admirable in other respects.

By this general lack of attention to physical beauty Old English poets do not mean to imply that Germanic noblewomen were not beautiful, but rather that beauty is not explicitly relevant to their place in society or to the themes of the literature. There is more attention to the beauty of women in religious narrative poetry,[25] in keeping with themes inherited from the Bible and hagiographical literature. In the saint's life *Juliana*, for example, in which the evil Heliseus lusts after the holy virgin saint, the crowd marvel at the beauty of Juliana's face: 'duguð wafode / on þære fæmnan wlite' (lines 162–3). In *Genesis B* Eve is described as 'idesa scenost, / wifa wlitegost' (lines 626–7) ['brightest of ladies, most beautiful of women']. It is notable, however, that in religious literature reference is often not so much to the looks of the woman as to a brightness (indicated by words like *scenost*) shining out from her, a brightness which suggests radiance of personality or inner spirit rather than, or as well as, physical beauty.

Kathleen Parker has recently argued persuasively that while many

[23] Paul Beekman Taylor, 'The Old English Poetic Vocabulary of Beauty', in *New Readings on Women*, ed. Damico and Olsen, pp. 211–21.
[24] Michael J. Swanton, '*The Wife's Lament* and *The Husband's Message*: A Reconsideration', *Anglia* 82 (1964), 269–90 (at p. 271).
[25] See my article '"No Sex Please"', p. 13.

critics take the physical beauty of the heroine of *Judith* for granted, there are no strong grounds for doing so. The words *torht* (line 157), 'radiant, illustrious', and *beorht* (lines 58, 254 and 340), 'bright, fair', which are applied to her, 'refer to an interior spiritual beauty, if they refer to beauty at all'.[26] *Torht* and *beorht* are used elsewhere in Old English poetry particularly in connection with the spiritual realm, describing God, paradise and Christianity. With reference to people, *torht* is used of the saintly Guthlac (*Guthlac B*, line 1295), and *beorht* of the Virgin Mary (*Elene*, lines 782 and 789) and the good Sarra (*Genesis A*, line 1828).

Another epithet that might be thought to refer directly to the beauty of Judith's person is *wundenlocc* (lines 77 and 103), though this word is applied to her in the scene where she kills the sleeping Holofernes, which hardly seems a time to describe her beauty. *Wundenlocc* has been understood to mean both 'curly-haired' and 'with braided locks'. An analogous term, *wundenfeax*, is applied to King Hrothgar's horse in *Beowulf*, line 1400, where the meaning must be 'with braided mane', and so perhaps in Judith the meaning should be 'with braided hair'. The connotations of *wundenlocc* are not clear, however, especially since, as Peter Lucas has pointed out, it was not usual in Anglo-Saxon England for women to have their hair uncovered.[27] But anyway *wundenlocc* seems to belong with *beagum gehlæste*, *hringum gehrodene* and *golde gefrætewod* as part of the vocabulary of adornment rather than referring to natural beauty. The same word is also used of the Bethulian people as a whole (line 325) at their time of triumph, in a context in which reference to their physical beauty would not seem very relevant. In its one other occurrence in the surviving poetic corpus, in *Riddle 26* (line 11), it also refers to a woman. *Riddle 26* is a poem in which, as elsewhere in the Old English riddles, noble-sounding language is exploited in a less than noble context.

In a previous publication (completed before I had read Parker's article) I noted that most of the terms used of Judith do not actually specify sexual attractiveness. I was disturbed by one adjective, however, *ælfscinu* (line 14), which I translated 'of elfin beauty', commenting that this epithet 'suggests a sense of the beguiling power of female beauty', though adding defensively, 'but without implying culpability on the part of the heroine'.[28] Parker plausibly – and literally – interprets

---

[26] Parker, 'Is the Old English *Judith* Beautiful?', p. 72.
[27] '*Judith* and the Woman Hero', pp. 19–20.
[28] '"No Sex Please"', p. 12.

ælfscinu as 'elfin bright', in which the 'elf' part suggests a supernatural, but not necessarily evil (or beguiling), quality, and the 'bright' part is associated with the same semantic field as that represented in *torht* and *beorht*;[29] that is, Parker sees *ælfscinu* like these other epithets as conveying inner qualities. And even were we unwilling to accept the full extent of Parker's thesis and insisted on taking the 'bright' words in *Judith*, including *ælfscinu*, as connoting physical as well as inner qualities (after all, the poet nowhere says that she *wasn't* beautiful), I would still argue that their emphasis is not specifically on Judith's sexual attractiveness but on the beauty of her whole being.

There are two notable respects in which Judith does not behave like the Germanic noblewoman of Old English poetic tradition. One is that she is not shown engaging in the definitive activity of the gracious dispensing of drinks at the feast, even though there is an important feast scene in the poem. But of course the feast scene in *Judith* is a riotous affair, one of whose functions is to establish the drunken uncouthness of Holofernes. The poet deliberately disassociates the noble Judith from this scene. Unlike in the biblical account, in which she consciously uses the feast as part of her seduction of Holofernes and also to get him as drunk and incapacitated as possible, Judith is not even present at the feast scene in the poem. There is no place for a gracious noblewoman at the disordered feast of Holofernes.

The other respect in which Judith is unlike Wealhtheow, the lady from *Maxims I* and other noblewomen in traditional Old English verse is, of course, that she is presented as taking on the male role of hero, with its violent action. She carries out an heroic act and we have seen that the poet applies male heroic vocabulary to her – she is *ellenrof*, *collenferhð* and so on – and highlights her role as a military leader. These are ways in which Judith might be regarded, in the gender-demarcated world of Old English poetry, as significantly masculinised. Mark Griffith speaks of the poet effecting means to 'masculinise and heroise Judith by the redirecting of gendered language'.[30] However, the masculinisation of Judith is also interestingly countered in the poem, as consciousness of her femaleness is consistently maintained. As has recently been pointed out, the female bond with her maidservant is

---

[29] Parker, 'Is the Old English *Judith* Beautiful?', p. 65.
[30] *Judith*, p. 69; see also Helen Damico, 'The Valkyrie Reflex in Old English Literature', in *New Readings on Women*, ed. Damico and Olsen, pp. 176–90: Damico argues that in general the treatment of Judith and of the other females in Old English heroic poetry 'corresponds closely to the treatment given the Old English heroic male warrior' (p. 182).

particularly highlighted,[31] and the poet insistently suggests that Judith is far from comfortable being a hero. In what is a sensitively gender-conscious portrayal of the protagonist, it is made clear that although she courageously takes the role of hero upon herself, this is a role not suited to her, as a woman, and one which she struggles anxiously to fulfil. That she succeeds is seen as truly a cause for the triumphant celebration at the end of the poem, when she is presented with the spoils of victory.

The heroic epithets applied to Judith are invariably accompanied by a feminising noun: she is *ides ellenrof* (lines 109 and 146), 'a valorous lady' and *mægð modigre* (line 334), 'a courageous woman', and the word *collenferhð*, 'brave-hearted', is applied, in a passage that recurrently balances heroic terminology with references to femininity, to both herself and her maidservant, both also being *ellenþriste*, 'boldly daring', and *eadhreðige*, 'triumphant':

> Eodon þa gegnum þanonne
> þa idesa ba,   ellenþriste,
> oðþæt hie becomon,   collenferhðe,
> eadhreðige mægð,   ut of ðam herige.   (lines 132–5)

[They went then directly, both of the ladies, boldly daring, until they arrived, the brave-hearted and triumphant ladies, out of the army.]

The heroic epithets are also accompanied by reference to Judith's wisdom, one of the qualities particularly associated with the ideal Germanic noblewoman.

Judith's role of military leader consists of encouraging the men of Bethulia in a speech before battle (lines 186–99) but not actually leading them into battle. Indeed, after making this speech she withdraws from the action, leaving the men to resume their normal role. And in the speech itself she is distinctly less assertive in her encouragement than Byrhtnoth or Hnæf would have been:

> Nu ic gumena gehwæne
> þyssa burgleoda   biddan wylle,
> randwiggendra   þæt ge recene eow
> fysan to gefeohte.   (lines 186–9)

---

[31] Mary Dockray-Miller, 'Female Community in the Old English *Judith*', *Studia Neophilologica* 70 (1998), 165–72.

[Now I wish to ask each of these townspeople, each shield-bearer, that you quickly hasten to the fight.]

The use of *biddan* is notable here, as Judith modulates in her address from command (*het*, line 171) to request. Lucas compares a similar use of *biddan* by Wealhtheow in *Beowulf*: 'Doð swa ic bidde' (line 1231), 'Do as I request'.[32]

In the lead-up to the scene in which she kills Holofernes she makes her way to the innermost place of danger, Holofernes's tent, but only when she is sent for (*het . . . fetigan*, 'ordered to fetch', lines 34–5) from the guest-chamber in which she has been waiting; and she is passively *brought* there (*lædan*, 'lead', line 42, *gebrohton*, 'brought', line 54, *gebroht*, 'brought', line 57) rather than striding forth heroically. Indeed, it is Holofernes's men who do the striding (*stopon*, 'advanced', line 39, *eodon*, 'went', line 55), and in this passage heroic vocabulary is applied to them (*stercedferhðe | hæleð*, 'stout-hearted warriors' at lines 55–6), not Judith, who is wise (*ferhðgleawe*, line 41, *snoteran*, line 55) and shining (*torhtan*, line 43, *beorhtan*, line 58), but seems to have no control over what is happening. She is speedily (*ofstum*, line 35, *hraðe*, line 37, *fromlice*, line 41, *snude*, line 55) delivered into the hands of the monstrous one.

In this passage Judith does not look like a hero. But appearances are deceptive here, for God is with her and she herself is clear-thinkingly mindful of the task in hand. When Holofernes slumps into a drunken sleep she thinks how she can most easily (*eaðost*, line 75) dispatch him before he wakes up. This shows her resolution but also a decidedly unheroic concern to do the job in the easiest way possible. Judith draws a sword and makes a prayer to the Almighty for victory and true faith, before killing Holofernes in his sleep. She grabs him by the hair and drags him into position for the kill, again trying to manœuvre his sleeping body as 'easily' as she can manage to: 'swa heo ðæs unlædan eaðost mihte / wel gewealdan' (lines 102–3), 'just as she could most easily manage the miserable one'. Grabbing an enemy by the hair would be an undignified tactic for a male hero (not to mention killing someone in his sleep), and it is shameful (*bysmerlice*, line 100) for Holofernes to be dragged in this way, but to Judith the important thing is resolutely (*eornoste*, line 108) to complete the deed and then quickly (*snude*, line 125) to get back to Bethulia. Even then she does not make a clean job of beheading Holofernes and has to take two goes at it (lines

---

[32] '*Judith* and the Woman Hero', p. 22.

103–11). A male hero like Beowulf would have succeeded at the first stroke, but then a male hero would not be pitted against a sleeping drunkard.

The prayer to the Almighty (lines 83–94) expresses strongly Judith's emotional agitation at the time of action. She is aware of the difficulty of the task, and exclaims,

> þearle ys me nu ða
> heorte onhæted   ond hige geomor,
> swyðe mid sorgum gedrefed.   (lines 86–8)

[My heart is now greatly worked up and my mind is troubled and much stirred with sorrows.]

And she refers again a few lines later, in the closing words of the speech, to that which is grievous in her mind (*torne on mode*, line 93) and hot in her breast (*hate on hreðre minum*, at line 94). In the speech she emphasises her need (*þearfendre*, line 85, *þearfe*, line 92) for God's help, a theme which had also been alluded to in the opening lines of the poem (at least, as the poem survives) (*þearfe*, line 3). The self-belief and confidence of the hero is lacking here, but Judith is guided by her faith in God (lines 6, 89 and 344), which enables her to carry out her daunting task. God watches over Judith throughout. When she first enters the tent where the licentious Holofernes is waiting for her, God is unwilling to permit (*geðafian*, line 60) that he should harm her and by means of the drunken swoon prevents him from the act (*he him þæs ðinges gestyrde*, line 60).

Judith needs the help of God, but she is more than a passive instrument in the poem, for she also shows resolution, courage and clear thinking at the time of crisis, and she has to carry out the violent deed with her own hands. She does not embrace her task with relish, but she acts *eornoste*, 'fiercely', and with determination.

Throughout the poem Judith's attitudes and 'instinctive' behaviour are presented as those of a Germanic noblewoman, even though her role is not that of a woman at all but of a hero. It is the discrepancy between the person and the role that gives particular interest to the characterisation of Judith and urgency to the narrative of her killing of Holofernes. Rather than minimising her difficulties in carrying out this act as a woman, the poet highlights her ostensible unsuitedness to the task, thereby magnifying all the more her faith and achievement.

Remembering Veronica in Anglo-Saxon England

MARY SWAN

Introduction: Saints, relics and women in the late Anglo-Saxon Church

SAINTS' CULTS GENERATED some of the most public, social and
organised activities of the Christian Church in Anglo-Saxon England.
Saints were invoked as patrons of new and existing churches; their
feast-days were celebrated each year by lay people, nuns and monks;
they were prayed to and sung to; shrines were established at the places
where they were buried, and people travelled to their shrines to pray
and to do homage; stories of their lives and miracles were recorded in
all kinds of art and in Old English and Latin literature produced in
England and imported to England from mainland Europe, were read by
high-status lay individuals as well as by nuns and monks, and were
heard by anyone who attended church on a saint's feast-day. A range of
evidence survives to tell us about this, in the form of manuscript texts
and images, stone and ivory carvings, written references to the
dedications of individual churches and to the celebration of saints'
days by particular churches.

Closely tied to the cult of saints is that of relics: material objects
believed to be either a part of the body of a saint, or a part of an
associated object.[1] Bodily relics included almost every imaginable part
of the skeleton, hair and nails; secondary relics ranged from pieces of
clothing to things related to the life and miracles of a particular saint,
such as earth from the spot at which the Anglo-Saxon king and saint,
Oswald, was killed. The acquisition and promotion of relics by a
religious community was often part of an elaborate politics of establishment, validation, and advancement by affiliation to a particular saint
or group of saints, and also, by extension, to other important religious
centres associated with them. Once a religious community could show
that it possessed significant relics, its chances of receiving further relics

---

[1] For a discussion of this subject, see David Rollason, *Saints and Relics in Anglo-
Saxon England* (Oxford: Oxford University Press, 1989) and Susan Ridyard, *The
Royal Saints of Anglo-Saxon England* (Cambridge: Cambridge University Press,
1988).

as gifts, and other endowments of money and land, were greatly increased. The recording in writing of lists of relics was one way to register a community's significance, and also its legitimate ownership of items associated with a particular saint, and thereby its appropriation of that saint.

The cult of relics was flexible and popular enough to accommodate sub-cults, and one of the most popular of these from the Early Middle Ages onwards was the cult of the 'Instruments of the Passion'; the objects, including the crown of thorns, lance, spear and sponge, with which Christ was tortured before his crucifixion. Popular and learned devotional focus on the Passion was one of the primary motivating forces behind the development of affective piety in the High and Late Middle Ages. This devotional movement is often identified by scholars as one of the most striking markers of the beginning of the High Middle Ages. It is described as a major shift in the conception of the relationship between the individual Christian and God, and is linked to a perceived development in Western Europe of a philosophical and psychologically-conceived notion of the individual from about the twelfth century onwards.

One of the most striking features of affective piety is its focus on the emotional and the physical as much as on the intellectual. Because of this, and because of its popularity amongst lay and religious women, scholars have identified it as a feminising movement which offers women believers the chance to create, through a deep concentration on the Passion, a devotional object – Christ – in their own image, as someone bleeding, powerless and subject to others.

The gendering of devotion and of religious politics is not, of course, absent from early medieval England. The presence of aristocratic women in positions of religious power in early Anglo-Saxon England is commonly observed by scholars. Perhaps the most famous example is that of Hild of Whitby, born in c.614 and connected to the royal houses of East Anglia and Northumbria, who was abbess of Hartlepool and Whitby and closely associated with senior monastic figures and events, including the Synod of Whitby.[2] Double houses like that of which Hild had charge at Whitby – religious establishments housing both monks and nuns (in separate areas) and ruled by an abbess – do not persist throughout the Anglo-Saxon period, however. By the mid-tenth century most of those which existed earlier had been closed

---

[2] See Michael Lapidge, 'Hild or Hilda', in *The Blackwell Encyclopaedia of Anglo-Saxon England*, ed. Michael Lapidge *et al.* (Oxford: Blackwell, 1999), p. 239.

down, or converted into men-only communities, ruled by abbots. Almost all Anglo-Saxon nunneries which survived into the tenth century, or which were founded then, were very closely connected to the West Saxon royal house and to the Benedictine Reform. These changes had a profound effect on the possibilities for women within the major sectors of the Christian Church in England; opportunities were reduced, and the number of women in formal religious communities greatly decreased.[3]

In the light of this restricting and policing of women's organised religious lives, it seems ironic that a particular feature of the Benedictine Reform – the political powerhouse of the later Anglo-Saxon Church – was its promotion of the most central female saint of all: the Virgin Mary; but then again, the Virgin Mary is hardly an example of unrestricted womanhood, and is also of course the ultimate impossible role model for women: a virgin mother.[4]

Despite a wide variety of surviving evidence, and the important scholarly work of recent years, the insights that we have into late Anglo-Saxon England and the detail of its ecclesiastical life are very selective. When working with texts, for example, it is still extremely hard to work out how to interpret isolated manuscript references to something we have almost no other surviving evidence for: we are always reliant on having some sort of access to a cultural context when we set about interpreting a text, and we are constantly reminded of just how complex the study of textual transmission can be. The elusive textual references which will form the focus of this essay's analysis are to Veronica: the woman known from the very Early Middle Ages onwards in stories related to that of the life of Christ, and popular from the High Middle Ages onwards, but apparently almost unknown in Anglo-Saxon England. An examination of the evidence for knowledge of Veronica in Anglo-Saxon England raises important questions about how we fill in gaps in our knowledge, and about how – and whether – we can extrapolate from a hint into a theory about devotional practices now mostly lost from sight.

[3] Essential reading on this subject is Sarah Foot, *Veiled Women* 2 vols (Aldershot: Ashgate Press, 2000), which draws together all of the evidence for female religious activity in Anglo-Saxon England and postulates the growth of alternative religious communities for women in the face of this decrease in 'official' female monastic houses.

[4] Mary Clayton, *The Cult of the Virgin Mary in Anglo-Saxon England* (Cambridge: Cambridge University Press, 1990) is the major scholarly study of the Virgin Mary's place in Anglo-Saxon devotion.

Veronica is not a typical saint. No narrative of her whole life (*vita*), or of her death (*passio*) exists, and she does not feature in any surviving Anglo-Saxon calendars of feast-days, nor in any prayers, nor in any church dedications. Narratives concerning her are, however, popular from the Early Middle Ages onwards, and her popularity is due to her association with the cult of the Instruments of the Passion. It might seem that Veronica's extensive currency in the later Middle Ages is a product of the increasing interest in affective piety, but the tantalising fragments of evidence for her association with the Instruments of the Passion in Anglo-Saxon England raises the possibility that neither Veronica as Passion relic-holder, nor affective modes of religious practice, were the invention of the twelfth century.

The Veronica Legend

The story of Veronica grew, along with much other narrative, out of the very popular *Gospel of Nichodemus*; an apocryphal account of the events between Christ's trial and the Harrowing of Hell.[5] The *Gospel of Nichodemus* has its origins in at least two independent narratives, the longer of which is the *Acta Pilati*. Throughout the late Classical and early medieval periods, the *Gospel of Nichodemus* – itself a composite and a filling-in of the detail of and the gaps between events narrated in the Gospels – generated many other narrative strands, in which elements of its contents were developed into freestanding stories. In his important analysis of the *Gospel of Nichodemus* and the legend of Veronica, Thomas Hall refers to these developments as 'subsidiary apocrypha' and to the process of their production as 'narrative accretion'.[6] Hall identifies this process as 'one of the most character-istic features of medieval apocrypha',[7] and as will become clear, narrative accretion in medieval apocrypha does not stop with the

---

[5] For a detailed account of the development of the *Gospel of Nichodemus* and its transmission in Anglo-Saxon England, see Thomas Hall's chapter in J. E. Cross, with Denis Brearley, Julia Crick, Thomas N. Hall and Andy Orchard, *Two Old English Apocrypha and their Manuscript Source: 'The Gospel of Nichodemus' and 'The Avenging of the Saviour'*, Cambridge Studies in Anglo-Saxon England 19 (Cambridge: Cambridge University Press, 1996), esp. pp. 6–58. In the account of the development of the legend which follows, I am indebted to Hall's careful analysis.

[6] Hall, in Cross *et al.*, *Two Old English Apocrypha*, pp. 58 and 59.

[7] Hall, in Cross *et al.*, *Two Old English Apocrypha*, p. 59.

creation of a new, freestanding story, but rather continues with the production of variant versions of the same story, and the welding together of separate narratives.

The earliest, Greek version of the Veronica legend dates from the fourth century, and centres around Abgar, the King of Edessa, who asks for Christ's help in curing an illness from which he is suffering.[8] Abgar's envoy to Christ also happens to be his personal painter, and he makes a painting of Christ's face for the King. Numerous variant versions of this story exist, and they each modify it slightly to include some or all of the following details: Christ himself gives his portrait to the King; this portrait develops into one not made by human hand; it acquires miraculous powers; and, most significantly for the purposes of this essay, a woman is introduced into the story. The first appearance of the woman is as a princess called Berenice who receives the image of Christ, and gradually Berenice gets identified with the woman in the gospels who is cured of bleeding by Christ after she touches the hem of his garment.[9]

Scholarship has shown that this legend is current in the West by the eighth century at the latest, when a narrative, known as the *Cura sanitatis Tiberii*, circulates as an appendix to the *Gospel of Nichodemus*. The *Cura sanitatis Tiberii* replaces Abgar with Tiberius, and has Tiberius, who is sick, send Volosianus to the East to look for Christ. Volosianus finds Veronica, a woman who was cured by Christ of a haemorrhage, and who has had a portrait of Christ painted. After some resistance by Veronica, Volosianus sees her painting and is inspired by it to vow to punish those responsible for Christ's death. Volosianus then returns to Rome with Veronica; Veronica shows her painting to Tiberius; he adores it, is healed and is baptised.

The legend of Veronica proper is known as the *Vindicta Salvatoris*, and is a development of the *Cura sanitatis Tiberii* which prefaces the story of Tiberius with another king's – Titus of Burgidala's – illness and miraculous cure. After being cured of a facial cancer, Titus sets off to find the portrait of Jesus which Veronica owns. As in the earlier *Cura sanitatis Tiberii*, Veronica is reluctant to part with the portrait, but

---

[8] This version of the story is recorded by Eusebius of Caesarea, in his *Historia ecclesiastica*. Hall gives a full account of all of the versions of the Veronica legend and their relationship to Anglo-Saxon texts, in Cross *et al.*, *Two Old English Apocrypha*, pp. 58–81.

[9] Matt. 9.20–2; Mark 5.25–34; Luke 8.43–8. Berenice is also the name given in the *Acta Pilati* to the woman cured of bleeding; see Hall in Cross *et al.*, *Two Old English Apocrypha*, p. 41.

eventually reveals it to Titus's emissary Volosianus who takes the portrait and Veronica back to Rome to present the portrait to Tiberius who adores it and is cured of his illness.

Of all the elements of this very accreted narrative it is, of course, this image of Christ's face which really takes off. A relic of this image of Christ has been kept in St Peter's, Rome, possibly from as early as the eighth century.[10] From the twelfth century onwards, the legend of the cure of the King and of Veronica's part in it becomes very popular in prose and poetry in many languages. In the twelfth century it is one of the sources of Jacobus de Voragine's *Legenda aurea* and of the *Kaiserchronik*. In the thirteenth century it is translated into Welsh, partly translated into Catalan, and adapted into Icelandic. Its Old and Middle French versions, known as the *Vengeance de Nostre-Seigneur*, were very popular from the thirteenth to the fifteenth centuries. Its description of the destruction of Jerusalem exerts an influence on many vernacular romances.[11] In the thirteenth century, feastdays for Veronica and for devotion to the relic image of Christ – the *vera icon* – are instituted; in 1208 Pope Innocent III establishes an annual procession in honour of the relic at St Peter's.

One of the most significant turns in the development of the legend is the merging of Veronica with another, para-biblical, person. She is still the woman Christ healed of bleeding, but she is now also one of the women of Jerusalem who are waiting on the road to Calvary, and – in the part of the legend most famous today – as Christ passes her, she wipes his face with a cloth, and the image of his face is imprinted on the cloth. This episode becomes so popular that it overtakes all the rest in the late medieval period and after, and features in many texts, including plays, and in countless paintings and sculptures. Scholarship has dated the introduction of this merging of the woman healed of bleeding and the woman who wipes Christ's face and ends up with his image on her cloth to no earlier than the fourteenth century,[12] but as

[10] See Alvin S. Ford, ed., *La Vengeance de Nostre-Seigneur. The Old and Middle French Prose Versions. The Version of Japheth* (Toronto: Toronto University Press, 1984), p. 12; *The Oxford Dictionary of Saints*, ed. David Hugh Farmer (Oxford: Oxford University Press, 1978), p. 389; and *New Catholic Encyclopedia* (New York, 1967), p. 625.

[11] For more detail of all of these versions, see Hall in Cross et al., *Two Old English Apocrypha*, pp. 80–1.

[12] See, for example, *New Catholic Encyclopedia*, p. 625 and *Dictionnaire d'archéologie chrétienne et de liturgie*, ed. F. Cabrol and H. Leclerq (Paris, 1950), vol. 15, cols 2963–4. The major study of the iconography of this episode is by Karl Pearson, *Die Fronica: Ein Beitrag zur Geschichte des Christusbildes im Mittelalter* (Strasburg, 1887).

will be shown by the examination of the Anglo-Saxon evidence which follows, the roots of this development might be much earlier than that.

The development of the Veronica legend may, then, be summarised as follows: the legend of Abgar gets amalgamated with the story of the bleeding woman and her cure; Abgar becomes Tiberius; the woman's name becomes Veronica; the portrait of Christ becomes the *vera icon*; Veronica becomes the woman who wiped Christ's face on the road to Calvary; and the *vera icon* becomes her miraculous cloth.

Veronica in Anglo-Saxon texts

Vindicta Salvatoris

Veronica is named in two Old English narrative texts. Both are copies of the *Vindicta Salvatoris*, and both presumably descend, either directly or via another Old English translation, from a Latin version, such as that contained in Saint-Omer, Bibliothèque Municipale, 202, which was written in western Flanders, probably at the monastery of Saint-Bertin, in the ninth century, and which contains Latin texts of the *Gospel of Nichodemus* and the *Vindicta Salvatoris*.[13] One Old English version is in Cambridge, University Library Ii. 2. 11, a manuscript which contains the West Saxon Gospels, the Gospel of Nicodemus and assorted Exeter-related documents.[14] The other is in Cambridge, Corpus Christi College 196, a large fragment of a martyrology. Both these manuscripts were written in the third quarter of the eleventh century, and CUL Ii. 2. 11 has been annotated by readers in the twelfth century. Both manuscripts were written at Exeter, which is, as will be seen, a particularly significant place for the development of traditions of Veronica in late Anglo-Saxon and early Anglo-Norman England.

The versions of the *Vindicta Salvatoris* in CUL Ii. 2. 11 and Corpus 196 are identical in almost every detail, except that the Corpus 196 version is incomplete: approximately its first tenth and the last quarter are missing. The narrative in these two Old English versions begins with a noble man called Tyrus who lives in Lybia and who has cancer of the face. The emperor Tiberius, who has leprosy, sends a man called Nathan to Rome on business. On the way, Nathan meets Tyrus, who

---

[13] See J. E. Cross and Julia Crick in Cross *et al.*, *Two Old English Apocrypha*, pp. 10–35.
[14] For details of all Old English manuscripts referred to, see N. R. Ker, *Catalogue of Manuscripts Containing Anglo-Saxon* (Oxford: Clarendon Press, 1957; re-issued with supplement, 1990).

asks him to look out on his travels for anything which might heal the sores on his face. Nathan says that he has heard of a prophet called Christ who was able to heal the sick, including a woman called Veronica – 'And sum wyf wæs þoligende blodes fleusan huru .XII. wynter, seo wæs Veronix genemned, and heo hym to genealæhte wydæftan hym and his hrægles fnædes æthran . . .'[15] – and who was crucified by the Jews. This information makes Tyrus believe in Christ, and he says that if he had been with Christ and had seen his face, he would have taken vengeance against Christ's enemies. At this, Tyrus' cancer is cured. Nathan baptises him and gives him the new name Titus. Titus sets out for Jerusalem with Vespasian, a fellow convert. They besiege the city, the people repent of their sins and hand over Jerusalem to Titus and Vespasian, who begin to look for any surviving relics of Christ. From this point, the story is similar to the other versions outlined above: Titus and Vespasian find a Christian woman called Veronica who has an image of Christ's face, and they tell Tiberius to send Volosianus to Judea. Tiberius tells Volosianus to look for someone who can heal him in the name of Christ. When he arrives in Jerusalem, Volosianus meets Joseph of Arimathea and Nicodemus and Veronica, who tells of how Christ healed her bleeding: '"þæt ic wat, þæt ða ic on þære mænige wæs þæs folces, þæt ic to him cuman ne myhte, buton þæs ic hys hrægles fnædes oðhran, and me þæs blodes fleusa huru twelf gear eglode, ic wæs þa sona hal geworden . . ."'.[16] Volosianus orders her to hand over her relic of Christ; she refuses and denies that she has it ('Veronix hym þa swyðe wyðsoc and sæde þæt heo nane halignyssa myd hyre næfde');[17] the relic is found and Volosianus sails back home with Veronica, who does not want to leave her relic ('"To soðon ic þe secge, gif þu hyne nelt me agyfan, ne forlæte ic næfre þe ærþon ðe ic geseo hwar þu hyne alecge . . ."').[18]

---

[15] From the CUL version. 'And there was a certain woman, who was called Veronica, suffering an issue of blood for twelve years, and she came up to Him from behind and touched the hem of His garment . . .': ed. and trans. Cross et al., Two Old English Apocrypha, p. 255, §6.
[16] '"I knew that I was in a crowd of people, and could not approach Him, except to touch the hem of His garment, and a flow of blood had afflicted me for twelve years, and I was immediately healed . . ."': Cross et al., Two Old English Apocrypha, p. 279, §22.
[17] 'Veronica then refused him firmly, and said that she did not have any holy relic with her': Cross et al., Two Old English Apocrypha, p. 281, §24.
[18] '"Truly I tell you, if you will not give Him up to me, I shall never leave you until I see where you have put Him . . ."': Cross et al., Two Old English Apocrypha, pp. 283–5, §26.

Tiberius looks at Veronica's relic and worships it: his leprosy is cured and he is baptised.

In 1996, scholarship on the Old English versions of the Veronica legend was greatly advanced by the publication and discussion of the Latin version of the *Vindicta Salvatoris* in Saint-Omer 202 by J. E. Cross, Denis Brearley, Julia Crick, Thomas Hall and Andy Orchard. Cross and his collaborators have identified annotations in Old English in Saint-Omer 202 which show that it was definitely in England – and probably in Exeter – for a period in the eleventh century during the episcopate of Leofric.[19]

This connection is very exciting, since Cross and his collaborators have identified a Latin text which is very close in narrative content to the two Old English copies, and which was for a time in the place where they were produced. Thomas Hall suggests that the two Old English copies are not direct translations from Saint-Omer 202, but rather that they are independent copies of the same earlier (and now lost) Old English translation, which was made from the Saint-Omer Latin text.[20]

It is clear when the CUL and Corpus OE versions are compared with the Saint-Omer Latin text that they are very close, but there are some differences of detail and expression which are important signs of how the two Old English versions might reflect elements of the legend specific to England in the eleventh century, and of how they relate to each other. The following three examples are suggestive of the relationship of the CUL text to the Corpus one:

1   (Cross *et al.*, *Two Old English Apocrypha*, pp. 254–5)
St-Omer 202   'aliam mulierem . . . nomine Veronicae, que accessit
                  retro ad eum' ['another woman, Veronica by name . . .
                  who came up to Him from behind']

---

[19] Cross *et al.*, *Two Old English Apocrypha*, pp. 4–5 and 31–5. Cross lists the three Old English annotations as *hordome*, an interlinear gloss over *fornicatione*; a pen trial *hwæt wyltu* in a margin, and a drawing of an animal labelled *wesend*. All three entries are in different hands, which leads Cross to the conclusion that they were made in England, rather than by Anglo-Saxon scribes working in Saint-Bertin, and that the manuscript was therefore in England for a time. Cross cites Malcolm Parkes's opinion that the *hwæt wyltu* pen-trial was written in the Exeter scriptorium during Leofric's episcopate, but also the views of others that 'the script is not that of a distinctively Exeter hand' (Cross *et al.*, *Two Old English Apocrypha*, pp. 7–8)

[20] Hall in Cross *et al.*, *Two Old English Apocrypha*, pp. 76–7.

CUL Ii. 1. 22   'sum wyf . . . Veronix genemned, and heo hym to genealæhte wyðæftan hym'
['a certain woman, who was called Veronica . . . and she came up to Him from behind']

Corpus 196   'nealæhte wyf æftan' for 'genealæhte wyðæftan'

These excerpts are from the account of Christ healing Veronica's bleeding. The Latin text has Veronica coming up behind Christ, and the CUL text has the same. The Corpus version, however, has 'nealæhte wyf æftan' where CUL has 'genealæhte wyðæftan'. This does more or less make the same sense as the CUL version, but it could easily be the result of the Corpus scribe mishearing the CUL text or a lost, identical, one, or possibly an example of haplography.

2   (Cross et al., *Two Old English Apocrypha*, pp. 262–3)

St-Omer   'cognoscant quia non est similis illi in terra'
['let them know that there is no-one like Him on earth']

CUL   'oncnawon þæt næfre on eorðan hys gelica ne gewearð'
['recognise that there has never been His like on earth']

Corpus   'gemacan' for 'gelica'
['make' for 'like']

The second example is another possible instance of mishearing. Titus is speaking to Vespasian, and he says that they should go to avenge Christ so that everyone shall know that there has never been anyone like him on earth. The Saint-Omer Latin text and the CUL version match each other here. The Corpus version, however, differs once again, and has 'gemacan' for CUL's 'gelica'. The only likely explanation for this is that the Corpus scribe was copying the Old English text by ear, not by eye, and that they lost attention and misheard 'gemacan' for 'gelica'.

3   (Cross et al., *Two Old English Apocrypha*, pp. 278–82)

St-Omer   'Viuit ipse Deus, morte morieris tu'
['God himself lives; you will die a death']

CUL   'Swa me se sylfa dryhten libbe, þam wyrsestan deaðe þu scealt sweltan'

	['As the Lord Himself lives; you shall die the worst death']
Corpus	'helpe' for 'libbe'
	['helps' for 'lives', giving, perhaps, 'As the Lord may help [me]']

This third example comes at the point where Volosianus is berating Pilate in Jerusalem. The Saint-Omer version has Volosianus asserting that God lives and that Pilate will die. The CUL version keeps the sense of this, but turns it from a short, balanced pair of oppositions to a sort of idiomatic intensifier. The Corpus version keeps the CUL intensifier structure, but changes 'libbe' to 'helpe', which makes the phrase sound like another, equally appropriate, stock phrase, but loses the rhetorical life/death opposition.

These examples, then, raise the possibility that the CUL text has been copied from a manuscript of the Old English translation of a Latin text very like that in Saint-Omer 202, and that the Corpus text has been copied from the dictation of an Old English translation – either that in CUL, or another, lost one. In any case, earlier, presumably continental, traditions of Veronica are here being both remembered and re-membered in eleventh-century Exeter.

There are also points where the Old English versions share differences from the Saint-Omer Latin:

4	(Cross *et al.*, *Two Old English Apocrypha*, pp. 270–3)
St-Omer	'Inueneruntque mulierem cui nomen erat Veronice et inuenerunt uultum domini cum ea.'
	['And they found a woman whose name was Veronica, and found the face of the Lord with her']
CUL/Corpus	'hig an wif fundon, þære nama wæs Veronix . . . and eac hyt wæs seo ylce Veronix, [þe] þæs hælendes reafes æthran . . . Heo wæs þa sumne dæl hæbbende of þam reafe þæs hælendes and hyt swyðe deorwyrðlice heold and eac heo hyt for Crystes andwlytan æfre hæfde'
	['they found a woman whose name was Veronica . . . because she was the same Veronica who had touched the Saviour's garment . . . She had a certain portion of the Saviour's garment, and held it in great honour, and kept it always because of Christ's face']

This example is from the part of the narrative where Titus and Vespasian find Veronica. The Saint-Omer text states that Veronica had with her the Lord's face. The CUL and Corpus versions, however, add a very significant detail: that Veronica had a piece of Christ's garment, and they seem to imply that the impression of Christ's face is on this piece of his garment, even though exactly how Veronica might have got the impression of Christ's face on to a piece of *his* garment is not made clear in either of the Old English versions.

5	(Cross *et al.*, *Two Old English Apocrypha*, pp. 280–1)
St-Omer	'uultum domini' ['the face of the Lord']
CUL/Corpus	'þæt hyt dryhtnes sylfes andwlyta wære . . . ac hyt wæs þæt reaf, þæt se sylfa hælend werede' ['that it was the face of the Lord himself . . . but it was the garment which the Saviour himself wore']

This example is from a slightly later point of the story, where Volosianus is asking Veronica to hand over her relic. The Saint-Omer text has him asking her for, and her handing to him, the face of the Lord, with no reference to a garment. The Old English texts, by contrast, have Vespasian ordering Veronica to hand over 'þa halignysse þe þu hæfst': 'that holy relic, which you have'. Volosianus is so amazed on seeing the image that he thinks that it is the face of the Lord himself – 'dryhtnes sylfes andwlyta' – but the narrator, in an unusual intervention, reminds us that in fact it was not Christ's face, but his garment: 'þæt reaf, þæt se sylfa hælend werede'. Here again, the Latin text does not refer to a garment, but the Old English versions are insistent upon the fact that that is what Veronica has in her possession.

6	(Cross *et al.*, *Two Old English Apocrypha*, pp. 290–1)
St-Omer	'miserunt inquisitionem de uultum domini et inuenerunt mulierem nomine Veronice qui pincxerat eum habens' ['they sent a search for the face of the Lord and found the woman, by name Veronica, holding it who painted it']
CUL	'se sæde þæt heo dryhtnes andwlitan hæfde' ['who said that she had the face of the Lord']

In the third example the Saint-Omer version describes Veronica as having *painted* a face of the Lord. The Old English version (the Corpus text has run out by this point, so CUL is the only witness) does not have any reference to her painting it: she simply has 'dryhtnes andwlitan'.

The differences between the Latin and the Old English versions examined above are strong indicators that the Veronica legend in eleventh-century England had a distinct twist: the CUL and Corpus texts show a connection being made between the image of Christ which Veronica possesses and a piece of his garment. This might merely be a garbling of her 'double' identity as the woman who touched Christ's garment, and the woman who has his image, but if so, it is not clear why such confusion should have crept in to the Old English texts, nor why they should both replicate it when in other instances they clear up apparent confusions in the Latin version. The tantalising possibility which these examples reveal is that by the eleventh century, there exists a distinctive, early, Old English tradition in which Veronica is already associated with an image of Christ's face which is not painted, but which is on a piece of cloth from a garment – a configuration very close to the story of her wiping his face with her veil, whose introduction scholars have dated to as late as the fourteenth century.

If this development of the legend is indeed already circulating in Old English texts in late Anglo-Saxon and early Anglo-Norman England, it is an indicator of the early stages of the movement towards affective piety in that it depicts a human figure enjoying a privileged relationship with Christ because she has possession of a piece of his clothing related to his Passion. This both makes the Veronica story more real and tangible, and makes Veronica herself more powerful as the owner of what would apparently be the one piece of Christ's clothing to survive his transfiguration. The question of this piece of Christ's garment and its relationship to the Veronica legend and to Anglo-Saxon England will be returned to at a later point in this essay.

As well as the CUL and Corpus texts, there is in fact a third Old English version of the *Vindicta Salvatoris*. This is in London, British Library, Cotton Vespasian D. xiv, written in the mid-twelfth century in Rochester or at Christ Church, Canterbury. One of the distinguishing features of Cotton Vespasian D. xiv is its dramatic editing of source texts to produce a set of readings on a variety of popular religious topics, and its *Vindicta Salvatoris* is not central to the discussion of traditions of Veronica in Anglo-Saxon England for one very good reason: it is heavily edited, and it omits all the sections of the narrative which mention Veronica.

This notwithstanding, the Cotton Vespasian *Vindicta Salvatoris* is interesting evidence for the complex ways in which this text seems to have been transmitted in England. There are some instances where the Cotton Vespasian version agrees more closely with the Saint-Omer text than do the CUL or Corpus versions, which raises the possibility that more, slightly 'variant', versions of the Saint-Omer text were in circulation in England, and that one of these might have been the ultimate source of the CUL and Corpus versions.

Despite Cross's note that the Cotton Vespasian version, apart from its omission of material, 'is scarcely a variant text' of the other Old English versions,[21] a number of significant differences between it and the CUL and Corpus versions give clues to the transmission of versions of the Veronica legend in England. Some instances are best explained by the Cotton Vespasian scribe working from memory, rather than from eye or ear as proposed above for the CUL and Corpus scribes.[22] These include Tyrus's expression of amazement at seeing people from Judea arriving in a ship, which reads '. . . þæt æfre Iudeisce men hyder on land myd scype sceolon cuman' ['that Jewish folk should come ashore here by ship'][23] in CUL and Corpus, but whose word-order in Cotton Vespasian is markedly different: '. . . þæt of Iudea lande scipen scolden hider cumen' ['that ships should come from the land of Judea'];[24] and Tyrus's subsequent order that the leader of the ship should come to him: the leader is described in CUL and Corpus as 'þone þe on þam scype yldost wære' ['the leader on the ship'],[25] but in Cotton Vespasian as 'se þe eldest wære on þan scipe' ['the one who was oldest (or most senior) on the ship'].[26]

In one instance, the Cotton Vespasian version appears to be tidying up the narrative duplication and complication produced in other Latin

---

[21] Cross et al., *Two Old English Apocrypha*, p. 135.

[22] For an analysis of the markers of Old English text reproduced from memory, see Mary Swan, 'Memorialised Readings: Manuscript Evidence for Old English Homily Composition', in *Anglo-Saxon Manuscripts and their Heritage*, ed. Phillip Pulsiano and Elaine Treharne (Aldershot: Ashgate Press, 1998), pp. 205–17.

[23] Cross et al., *Two Old English Apocrypha*, p. 251, §3.

[24] Bruno Assmann, *Angelsächsische Homilien und Heiligenleben*, Bibliothek der angelsächsischen Prosa 3 (Kassel: G. H. Wigland, 1889; reprinted with a supplementary introduction by Peter Clemoes, Darmstadt: Wissenschaftliche Buchgesellschaft, 1964), p. 193, ll. 16–17.

[25] Cross et al., *Two Old English Apocrypha*, pp. 251–3, §4.

[26] Assmann, *Angelsächsischen Homilien und Heiligenleben*, p. 193, ll. 19–20.

and Old English versions of the story by the double Tiberius/Titus episodes. The CUL and Corpus versions match the Saint-Omer version in that the second of these episodes is introduced by Tyrus's name being changed to Titus when he is baptised;[27] in Cotton Vespasian, no name-changing is necessary, since Tyrus takes his brother Titus along on his campaign in Jerusalem.[28] Perhaps here the sources of all three Old English versions contain a rather complex doubling, possibly that which survives in the CUL and Corpus versions, and the adaptor of the Cotton Vespasian version is rationalising it by introducing a second character to bear the second name.

At several points, all three Old English versions of the text agree with each other against the Latin of Saint-Omer, which strengthens the case for the Saint-Omer version not being the direct source of any of them, and for the existence in Anglo-Saxon England of an intermediate version or versions in Latin or Old English on which the Old English versions draw. The picture is complicated even further by the instances where the Cotton Vespasian version agrees more closely with the Saint-Omer text than do the CUL or the Corpus versions, including its simple 'Tirus þa cwæð' ['Tyrus then said'],[29] which matches the Saint-Omer 'Tyrus dixit' ['Tyrus said'], but does not agree with the CUL and Corpus versions, both of which give 'axode and hym to cwæð' ['answered him and said'].[30] As Andy Orchard notes, here the CUL and Corpus versions are expanding a phrase in a formulaic style typical of their translation strategies.[31] Another ex-ample of agreement of the Cotton Vespasian and Saint-Omer versions against CUL and Corpus is the Cotton Vespasian description of Tyrus being 'swa strang, swa he wæs þa, þa he wæs þrittig wintre' ['as strong as he was when he was thirty years old'].[32] There is no equivalent description in either the CUL or the Corpus versions, but the Saint-Omer text describes Tyrus's recovery with a similarly age-related simile: 'restitua est caro eius sicut caro pueri paruuli' ['his flesh . . . was restored like the flesh of a small boy'].[33] These instances where the Cotton Vespasian version is closer to the Saint-Omer one than are CUL and Corpus raises the possibility that other, slightly 'variant'

---

[27] Cross et al., *Two Old English Apocrypha*, pp. 260–61, §10.
[28] Assmann, *Angelsächsischen Homilien und Heiligenleben*, p. 194, l. 35.
[29] Assmann, *Angelsächsischen Homilien und Heiligenleben*, p. 194, l. 25.
[30] Cross et al., ed., *Two Old English Apocrypha*, pp. 252–53, § 5.
[31] In Cross et al., *Two Old English Apocrypha*, pp. 108–30, esp. p. 117.
[32] Assmann, *Angelsächsischen Homilien und Heiligenleben*, p. 194, l. 32.
[33] Cross et al., ed., *Two Old English Apocrypha*, p. 258, §9.

versions of the Saint-Omer text were in circulation in England, that one of these might have been the ultimate source of the CUL and Corpus versions, and that another, different one might have been the direct or indirect source of the Cotton Vespasian version.

As noted above, the Cotton Vespasian version of the *Vindicta Salvatoris* is edited to remove some of the narrative repetitions. Its most striking feature, however, is the excision of all of the sections which mention Veronica so that here her legend is dismembered. The effect of this is to render the story less dramatic and less miraculous: Tiberius's cure is here the result of Christian instruction and persuasion, rather than of the sight of the image of Christ's face. It also means that we have no witness to the transmission of the Veronica legend narrative in the *Vindicta Salvatoris* in Old English apart from the CUL and Corpus versions. It is in fact triply ironic that the Veronica sections are omitted from the Cotton Vespasian text: firstly because Cotton Vespasian D. xiv contains many other hagiographical texts, and so its compiler and presumably its intended readership/audience were interested in narratives about saints; secondly because we know that Veronica was becoming a particularly central character in the legend from the twelfth century onwards in other countries; and thirdly (and especially) because a prayer added to the end of Cotton Vespasian D. xiv implies that it was in the possession of a woman by the end of the twelfth century.[34] The excision of the Veronica sections of the *Vindicta Salvatoris* might imply that Cotton Vespasian D. xiv's original intended audience was not female, even if a later reader or owner was.

The Cotton Vespasian version of the *Vindicta Salvatoris* seems to show Veronica disappearing from view after the Conquest almost as soon as she surfaces in late Old English textual culture. There are, however, other traces of her, albeit very faint ones, from Anglo-Saxon England which might indicate a wider cultural context for her fame.

Charms and recipes

London, British Library, Royal 12 D. xvii was written in the mid-tenth century, probably at Winchester. It contains three collections of

---

[34]   This prayer to the Virgin Mary is added in a blank space in the manuscript, and its subject is identified as 'ego ancilla tua' ['I, your handmaid']. I suggest elsewhere that this might be a reference to a female vowess; see Mary Swan, 'Constructing Readerships for Post-Conquest Old English Manuscripts', in *Imagining the Book*, ed. John Thompson and Stephen Kelly (forthcoming, Turnhout: Brepols, 2002).

medicinal recipes, one of which includes the following details on fol. 53r:

Eft sceal mon swigende þis writan 7 don þas word swigende on þa winstran breost 7 ne ga he in on þæt gewrit ne in on ber . 7 eac swigende þis on don . HAMMANY^OEL . BRONICE . NOY^OEWTAY^OEPT.[35]

This recipe is for 'lencten adle', tertian fever. Instructions for the preparation of assorted herbs, the pouring of holy water and the singing of masses over them are given. The reader is then instructed to drink the mixture and to say the names of the evangelists, which are followed in the manuscript by different configurations of crosses, presumably meant to resemble some sort of secret writing, and then by apparently random series of runes. Then, in the excerpt reproduced above, the reader is instructed to write on their breast the words 'HAMMANYOEL. BRONICE': 'EMMANUEL, VERONICA', which are written in Greek characters in the manuscript. It is interesting that Veronica's name is here spelled 'Bronice', as this makes it look much more like the Berenice in the early medieval Greek versions of the legend. Beyond that, however, it is hard to say exactly what this recipe reveals about Veronica in Anglo-Saxon England, except that her name could have mysterious magic, curative properties, and that clearly one scribe at least knew it, and perhaps expected the readers to recognise it too. It is possible that Veronica is also referred to at one other point slightly earlier in this manuscript; in the charm on fol. 52v more Greek characters, whose function is to protect against evil witches and elvish tricks, have been suggested by G. Storms to read 'BeppNNIKNETTANI' ['Veronica'?].[36]

Veronica's name also appears to feature in some Anglo-Latin recipes in London, British Library, Royal 2 A. xx, 'The Royal Prayerbook', which was written in the first half of the tenth century, possibly in the Worcester region. Royal 2 A. xx contains a series of charms to staunch

---

[35] 'Again, a man shall in silence write this, and silently put these words on the left breast, and let him not go in doors with that writing, nor bear it in doors. And also in silence put this on. EMMANUEL, VERONICA.' Edited and translated in T. Cockayne, *Leechdoms, Wortcunning and Starcraft of Early England*, Rolls Series, 3 vols (London, 1864–66), II:140–1.

[36] G. Storms, ed., *Anglo-Saxon Magic* (The Hague, Nijhoff, 1948; repr. Folcroft, PA: Folcroft Library Editions, 1975), pp. 268–9. See also Michelle Brown's discussion of this charm in *Anglo-Saxon Manuscripts* (London: British Library Publications, 1991), p. 32.

bleeding, two of which invoke 'Beronice',[37] and which appear to associate Veronica with the woman cured of bleeding. Royal 2 A. xx also contains the Gospel extract on the woman with the flow of blood, and Michelle Brown has suggested that the manuscript may have been owned by a female physician in a nunnery.[38]

Veronica in Anglo-Saxon Art

A painting or sculpture from Anglo-Saxon England would, of course, be the most conclusive evidence of all for an Anglo-Saxon tradition of Veronica wiping Christ's face with a piece of cloth – whether his or hers – on which his image is imprinted. Although Anglo-Saxon manuscript illustrations of the Instruments of the Passion do exist,[39] and thus support the case for the status of the Passion and its narrative details as a devotional topic in later Anglo-Saxon England, no surviving images from Anglo-Saxon England have been securely identified with Veronica.[40] The female figure on one piece of stone

[37] Storms, *Anglo-Saxon Magic*, pp. 292–3.
[38] Brown, 'Female Book-Ownership and Production in Anglo-Saxon England: the Evidence of Ninth-Century Prayerbooks', in *Lexis and Text in Early English: Studies Presented to Jane Roberts* (Amsterdam: Rodopi, 2001), pp. 45–67 (p. 57).
[39] Both the Galba or Æthelstan Psalter and the Benedictional of Æthelwold include depictions of the Instruments of the Passion. The Galba Psalter, London, British Library, Cotton Galba A. xviii, whose illustration of the Instruments of the Passion is on fol. 2v, was written in the second half of the ninth century, probably near Liège, and is subsequently associated with Old Minster, Winchester. For details of this manuscript, see Phillip Pulsiano, 'Psalters', in *The Liturgical Books of Anglo-Saxon England*, ed. Richard W. Pfaff, Old English Newsletter *Subsidia* 23 (Kalamazoo, MI: Medieval Institute Publications, 1995), pp. 61–85 (p. 68). The Benedictional of Æthelwold, London, British Library, Add. 49598, whose illustration of the Instruments of the Passion is on fol. 9v, was commissioned by Bishop Æthelwold of Winchester (963–84). For a detailed account of this manuscript, see Robert Deshman, *The Benedictional of Æthelwold* (Princeton: Princeton University Press, 1995), and for discussion of the Instruments of the Passion illustrations in both manuscripts, see Deshman, *Benedictional of Æthelwold*, pp. 63–7.
[40] This is despite Hall's passing remark that Veronica 'is depicted with her miraculous cloth in at least two Anglo-Saxon manuscript illuminations' (Cross et al., *Two Old English Apocrypha*, p. 78). Hall gives a footnote reference to Pearson, *Die Fronica*, 'p.73 and table 18', which says that Pearson 'discusses the depictions of Veronica in the Benedictional of St Æthelwold and in an eleventh-century psalter'. In fact, on page 73 of his study, Pearson notes that Veronica's cloth is *absent* from the Benedictional of Æthelwold and an

sculpture, the Rothbury Cross Shaft, has in the past been described as
the woman being healed of the issue of blood, along with the cure of
the blind man, but Jane Hawkes's recent re-examination of this image
has led her to suggest that it is in fact a depiction of Martha at the
raising of Lazarus.[41] This modern scholarly identification of both
Veronica and Martha is perhaps in fact an unconscious mirroring of
an earlier tendency to confuse the two women, which might mean that
images such as that on the Rothbury Cross Shaft could have signified
both women by a single figure.[42]

Exeter, relics, and the tradition of Veronica

There are no other Anglo-Saxon textual references to Veronica, but
there is one piece of evidence which amplifies the link between the
particularly English version of her legend discussed above, and Exeter,
the place of composition of the CUL and Corpus manuscripts, and the
possible place in which Saint-Omer 202 received its Old English
annotations.[43] In manuscript Oxford, Bodleian Library, Auct. D. 2.
16, in a section written in the second half of the eleventh century on
folios added to a ninth- or tenth-century Breton gospels, is a list in Old
English of donations made by Æthelstan to the minster of St Mary and

eleventh-century Anglo-Saxon psalter. Pearson does indeed refer the reader at
this point to 'Tafel achtzehn', but his book contains no tables, so 'tafel' here
must translate as 'plate', and there is a plate 18. This plate, however, does not
clarify things, since it is a sixteenth-century engraving of Saints Peter and
Paul holding Veronica's cloth. I suspect, therefore, that Pearson's reference to
plate 18 was misplaced by his printers (he has no plates of any early medieval
illustrations), and that this error has been compounded in a complex series of
modern textual transmissions: firstly, somebody mistranslated Pearson's assertion that the Anglo-Saxon manuscripts do *not* contain images of Veronica,
and also mistranslated 'tafel' as 'table'; then this reference is repeated, and
picked up by Hall as evidence for Anglo-Saxon illustrations of Veronica and
her cloth.

[41] Jane Hawkes, 'The Miracle Scene on the Rothbury Cross-Shaft', *Archaeo-
logia Aeliana*, 5 (1989), 207–11 (at p. 208). It is interesting to note the possible
representation of the Instruments of the Passion on the Rothbury Cross head:
see Deshman, *Benedictional of Æthelwold*, p. 63, note 44.

[42] See Farmer, *Oxford Dictionary of Saints*, p. 389, who notes that 'Some . . .
identified [Veronica] . . . with Martha'.

[43] On later Anglo-Saxon Exeter, see Patrick W. Conner, *Anglo-Saxon Exeter:
A Tenth-Century Cultural History* (Woodbridge: Boydell & Brewer, 1993) and
'Exeter's Relics, Exeter's Books', in *Essays on Anglo-Saxon and Related Themes in
Memory of Lynne Grundy*, ed. Jane Roberts and Janet Nelson (London: King's
College Medieval Publications, 2000), pp. 117–56.

St Peter, Exeter, in the 930s. This includes grants of land, books and assorted relics, amongst which is a piece of Christ's garment: 'Of þam gyrlan þe ure drihten silf on him hæfde þa þa her on worulde betwix mannum wæs'.[44]

A Latin version of the Exeter relic-list in Oxford, Bodleian Library, Bodley 579 – one of a series of additions made in England, probably in Exeter, in the eleventh century to a late ninth- to early tenth-century missal written in North-East France and given to Exeter Cathedral by Bishop Leofric in the third quarter of the eleventh century – includes a matching, but shorter entry: 'De uestimento Domini'.[45] This entry also appears in London, British Library, Royal 6. B. vii, a late eleventh-century copy of Bodley 579, and in Exeter Cathedral Library 2861, a later twelfth-century version of the Latin relic-list.[46]

Of course, relic-fragments of cloth are nothing unusual, and indeed the Æthelstan list also includes fragments of the garment and the headdress of the Virgin Mary and of the clothes of St John.[47] In the light of the apparent existence of a distinctive Anglo-Saxon tradition about Christ's garment as witnessed by the eleventh-century CUL and Corpus manuscripts, however, it is tempting to speculate that this Exeter relic of Christ's garment might be in some way connected to the legend of Veronica. Another suggestive connection is the inclusion in the Exeter relic-lists of relics of Christ's cross and blood, and of the lance which pierced his side at the Crucifixion, which situate the garment-relics in the context of the Passion relics with which, I argue, Veronica was firmly associated in the later Anglo-Saxon period.[48]

Conclusion: Veronica in Anglo-Saxon England

The patchiness of the narrative evidence for Veronica in late Old English texts does not support the assumption that the Veronica legend

---

[44] W. Dugdale, *Monasticon Anglicanum*, 3 vols (London, 1817–30), II:528. Ed. and transl. Conner, *Anglo-Saxon Exeter*, pp. 178–9: 'From the garment which our Lord himself had on when he was here in the world among men'.

[45] Conner, *Anglo-Saxon Exeter*, p. 193. 'From the clothing of Christ'. Conner notes that blank space, sufficient for approximately eighteen characters, is unfilled at the beginning of the line for this entry, but it is not clear whether or not this might have been intended for more details of Christ's garments, as are given in the Old English list.

[46] See Conner, *Anglo-Saxon Exeter*, pp. 171 and 201.

[47] Conner, *Anglo-Saxon Exeter*, pp. 178–9.

[48] See Conner, *Anglo-Saxon Exeter*, pp. 178–9, 192 and 201.

was a dramatic, sudden introduction into England in the decades around the Conquest: if this were so, it is likely that much stronger contextual evidence for the introduction of her story would exist, in the form of other references, and also that signs would survive of the immediate continuation of the transmission of the story, rather than its apparent shutting-down in the Cotton Vespasian text. It is more likely, therefore, that the late Old English references in the CUL and Corpus texts, in conjunction with the relic-list evidence discussed above, mark a particular, Exeter, interest in working up the Veronica story from already-known elements – of which faint echoes can be seen in the charms references, where she is associated with bleeding, as is Christ at the Crucifixion – to suit a particular ecclesiastical establishment and its wish to promote its relic collection. The accepted popularity in the later Middle Ages of the legend of the miraculous imprint of Christ's face made on Veronica's cloth on the road to Calvary is perhaps not, then, a new development in this long and complex body of narrative, but rather a re-introduction of a story which was, in fact, already circulating in at least part of England in the latter part of the eleventh century.

'Born to Thraldom and Penance': Wives and Mothers in Middle English Romance

DAVID SALTER

> Wommen are born to thraldom and penance,
> And to been under mannes governance.
> Geoffrey Chaucer,
> The Man of Law's Tale (286–7)

Romance: A Feminine Genre?

NEAR THE BEGINNING of Book II of Chaucer's *Troilus and Criseyde*, during the first encounter that we witness between Criseyde and her uncle, Pandarus, there is a brief but characteristically witty exchange between the two characters that offers us a tantalising glimpse of contemporary responses to romance, and the ways in which those responses were bound up with, and shaped by, prevailing attitudes towards women. Chaucer tells us that Pandarus – searching for his niece – finds her with two female companions listening to a maid reading from the story (or 'geste') of the siege of Thebes. Criseyde informs her uncle that 'This romaunce is of Thebes that we rede' (100),[1] and she then proceeds to tell him of the death of King Layus at the hands of his son, Edippus, as well as of the last incident that had been read to them – the descent into hell of the 'bisshop' Amphiorax. Pandarus responds to his niece's brief rendering of the story by claiming to know it himself. But whereas Criseyde refers quite explicitly to '*this romaunce*', and describes a series of episodes unique to the vernacular, romance versions of the story, Pandarus cites as his source the 'bookes twelve' (108) of Statius's first-century Latin epic, the *Thebaid*, the classical account from which the medieval *Roman de Thèbes* is derived.[2]

---

[1] Geoffrey Chaucer, *Troilus and Criseyde*, Book II, Line 83, in Larry D. Benson et al., ed., *The Riverside Chaucer* (Oxford: Oxford University Press, 1987). All subsequent quotations from Chaucer's work will be from this edition.

[2] For an edition of the twelfth-century Old French *Roman de Thèbes* (the earliest known version of the story in the vernacular), see Raynaud de Lage, ed., *Le Roman de Thèbes*, 2 vols (Paris, 1966–7). An excellent translation of the *Thebaid* has recently been published by the Clarendon Press. See Statius, *The*

Although this episode is both brief and somewhat incidental to the main action of the scene – the attempt by Pandarus to persuade Criseyde to accept Troilus as her lover – it can, if carefully interpreted, tell us much about contemporary attitudes towards romance. As Paul Clogan notes, by alluding to the *Thebaid*, Pandarus is able to demon-strate his knowledge of a more authoritative and culturally prestigious version of the story than the one known to Criseyde.[3] Pandarus's allusion to the *Thebaid* can thus be seen as an assertion of the dominance of the ancient over the contemporary, of Latin over the vernacular, and of the genre of epic over that of romance. So Pandarus would seem to be engaged in a game of point scoring with his niece, but one that – as Susan Crane reminds us – is as much about gender as it is about genre.[4] For those authoritative, cultural forms with which Pandarus aligns himself were regarded as masculine in nature, while Chaucer presents the vernacular realm of romance as both literally and metaphorically an exclusively female domain (a suggestion seemingly confirmed by the Nun's Priest's famously dismissive description of 'the book of Launcelot de lake' as a text 'that wommen holde in ful greet reverance'). Whatever the actual gender composition of the romance audience, then, it would seem that, as Crane has claimed, the genre itself was perceived to be quintessentially feminine.[5] Moreover, it could be argued that the comparatively low cultural status that Pandarus ascribes to romance was determined, at least in part, by the prevailing anti-feminism of the time.

But, if we accept that romance is indeed a feminine genre, we are nonetheless presented with something of a paradox, for what seems to confront us when we examine romance is a feminine genre with virtually no female heroines. The massive preponderance (particularly in Middle English romance) of male heroes can be attested simply by turning to any anthology or bibliography of the genre, and listing a selection of the titles that we find there: *Sir Gawain and the Green Knight, Sir Orfeo, Sir Isumbras, Sir Gowther, Amis and Amiloun, King Horn, Kyng Alisaunder, Torrent of Portyngale, Sir Tristrem, Ywain and*

Thebaid, trans. A. D. Melville (Oxford, 1992). This episode from *Troilus and Criseyde* has been subject to a detailed analysis by Paul Clogan in his study 'Criseyde's Book of the Romance of Thebes', *Hebrew University Studies in Literature and the Arts* 13 (1985), 18–28.

[3] Clogan, 'Criseyde's Book of the Romance of Thebes', pp. 26–7.

[4] Susan Crane, *Gender and Romance in Chaucer's Canterbury Tales* (Princeton: Princeton University Press, 1994), p. 10.

[5] Crane, *Gender and Romance in Chaucer's Canterbury Tales*, p. 10.

Gawain, Sir Percyvell of Gales, Sir Degaré, and so on. That the title of each of these romances is derived from the name of its hero (or heroes) is a reflection of the strongly masculine bias or orientation of the genre as a whole. With just a few notable exceptions – the tales of Constance and Griselda, and their various analogues – Middle English romance is a genre that deals almost exclusively with male concerns, and that puts male experience at the centre of its universe.

Of course, this is not to say that women do not figure at all in Middle English romance. Rather, it is to note that they almost always play a secondary or supporting role, and one that is both defined and determined by the central male figure. So women tend to be presented not so much as protagonists in their own right, but as the mothers, wives, sisters, and lovers of the protagonist. And the precise nature of the parts played by women in romance comes into still sharper focus when we consider the kind of narratives with which we are concerned. Of the sample of twelve reasonably representative romances listed above, all but two – *Sir Orfeo* and *Sir Isumbras* – deal with the growth and development of young men, and their emergence from a state of dependence on authoritative, parental figures, into a life of autonomy and independence. As Derek Brewer remarks, romances are typically 'stories that are about being young and growing up' – a rite of passage that is given a distinctly gendered inflexion in Middle English romance.[6] For in this genre, the hero's journey from childhood to the adult world almost always involves a transfer of love and loyalty from one woman to another, as he loosens the intense emotional bond that ties him to his mother (or to some other maternal figure), and establishes in its place a new relationship with the woman, who, in the fullness of time, will become his wife.

While to a great extent Middle English romance does tend to marginalise female experience, it nonetheless acknowledges the centrality of women in moulding and developing the identity of the male hero. And it is particularly through their roles as wives and mothers that women in romance are able to accomplish this shaping of male identity. Of course, in the world of romance, just as in that of day-to-day experience, the roles of wife and mother cannot always be neatly separated, and the combination of marriage and motherhood frequently leads to conflicts of interest. For the mother of the romance hero, when married, often finds that the conjugal

[6] Derek Brewer, *Symbolic Stories: Traditional Narrative and the Family Drama in English Literature* (Cambridge: D. S. Brewer, 1980), p. 74.

obligations she owes her husband clash with the love and loyalty she bears her son.

Because marriage and motherhood are the two aspects of women's lives that are given by far the most prominence in Middle English romance, I shall explore in the pages that follow some of the different ways in which wives and mothers are represented in the genre. Of course, the criteria employed by romance for evaluating the actions of wives and mothers are not gender neutral; women tend to be judged on whether they are good wives and mothers *to* their respective husbands and sons. So we find that in romance, even those very restricted roles and identities that are available to women tend to be governed by masculine codes and concerns.

Rather than exploring the representation of marriage and mother-hood across a range of romance narratives, my analysis will concentrate in detail on just two texts that offer radically different visions of these two female roles. The first of these, the anonymous fourteenth-century Middle English romance, *Octavian*, is in many ways unexceptional, both in terms of its overall narrative structure, and more particularly in its treatment of women within its highly conventional narrative form.[7] And it is precisely because it is so representative – because it provides such a typical portrayal of female virtue and nobility – that I have decided to use it. However, in stark contrast to the conventional, and extremely laudatory image of female virtue and nobility that is presented in *Octavian*, the second of the two texts to which I shall turn, which tells of the miraculous conception of Alexander the Great, takes a much less sympathetic, more openly misogynistic line in its treatment of women. In terms of the sheer scale of his achievements, and the almost superhuman nature of his ambition, the biography of Alexander the Great (356–323 BC) has much in common with a romance narrative, and it was principally through a massively popular but highly fictitious romance that Alexander's life and deeds came to be known in the Middle Ages.[8] Throughout his adult life, the historical Alexander had an extremely intense and emotionally troubled rela-tionship with his mother, Olympias, which gave rise to his well-known remark, reported by the Greek historian, Arrian, that 'she was charging him a high price for his nine months' lodging in her womb'.[9] Just as

---

[7] See below, pp. 45–51.

[8] See below, pp. 51–54

[9] Arrian, *The Campaigns of Alexander*, trans. Aubrey de Sélincourt (Harmonds-worth: Penguin, 1971), Book 7, p. 368.

Olympias elicited ambivalent feelings in Alexander himself, as well as in the Greek and Roman historians who wrote about his life, so the medieval romances of Alexander find her a deeply troubling presence. The romance version of Alexander's miraculous conception and birth, which tells of Olympias's adulterous union with an Egyptian pharaoh who disguises himself as a dragon, and which is reported with a mixture of prurient horror and erotic fascination, provides a strikingly alternative vision of femininity to the comparatively anodyne account of wifely and maternal constancy that we find in *Octavian*. By exploring these two highly polarised representations of marriage and motherhood – the one deeply conventional, the other extraordinarily idiosyncratic – I hope to offer an account of women in medieval romance that suggests the full range of emotional responses that the genre allows them to command.

Octavian

Octavian is a romance that is intensely preoccupied with, and whose very narrative structure revolves around, the sometimes-conflicting bonds of love and loyalty that unite wives and husbands, and mothers and sons. As mentioned above, the romance offers what is in many ways an extremely conventional treatment of marriage and motherhood, and it is this unexceptional or exemplary quality – rather than any excellence or singularity on its part – that justifies its inclusion here.

Octavian was widely known throughout Europe during both the later Middle Ages and the early modern period, with versions surviving in English, French, Italian, German, Icelandic, and Polish.[10] The romance exists in two different Middle English forms, which both date from around the middle of the fourteenth century, and which are both thought to derive independently from the same Old French source. Of the two, which are known as the Northern and Southern versions, the former is widely regarded as the more coherent and artistically successful, and it is to this version of the romance that I shall refer throughout.[11] As *Octavian* is one of the less well-known Middle English

[10] Frances McSparren discusses the dissemination of *Octavian* in the introduction to her edition of the romance. See *Octavian*, ed. Frances McSparren, Early English Text Society, Original Series 209 (Oxford: Oxford University Press, 1986), pp. 40–1.

[11] The Northern *Octavian* is thought to have been composed either in the

romances, I shall preface my analysis of the poem with a brief summary of its rather complex and convoluted plot.

After seven years of a loving but childless marriage to his beautiful, virtuous (and unnamed) wife, the Emperor of Rome, Octavian, feels great sadness because of his failure to produce an heir. However, he is comforted by his wife, the Empress, who suggests that they dedicate an abbey to the Blessed Virgin Mary, in the hope that she will intercede with her son on their behalf. The abbey is duly established, and in the fullness of time the Empress gives birth to twin sons. But the couple's happiness is short-lived. Octavian's wicked mother, motivated purely by malice, is able to convince her son that the twins are illegitimate, and so in the erroneous belief that the Empress is an adulteress, and that his children are bastards, Octavian condemns them to death by burning. The Empress accepts her fate with stoical resignation, and prepares for death by praying for her two children to the Virgin Mary. But moved by pity for his wife, Octavian commutes her sentence to banishment, abandoning her and the two children in a wild and deserted forest on the border of his kingdom.

Having thus been left in the wilderness to fend for herself, the Empress suffers the further misfortune of having one of her children carried off into the forest by an ape. Then, while she is lying in a swoon, incapacitated from the shock, her other child is abducted by a lioness, eager to feed the boy to her cubs. But the lioness, still holding the child in her mouth, is in turn attacked and lifted into the air by a griffin. The lioness – along with the young child – is carried off to a remote island, and as soon as she is placed back on the ground, she fights and kills the monstrous beast. Then, in a complete reversal of her original intention, she lies down next to the boy, and begins to suckle him.

Meanwhile, the Empress, distraught at the loss of her two children, but accepting her fate as divinely ordained, resolves to go on a pilgrimage to Jerusalem, to which end she boards a ship that happens

North East Midlands, or slightly further to the north, and survives in two manuscripts dating from the fifteenth century: Lincoln, Dean and Chapter Library, 91 (the Lincoln Thornton manuscript), and Cambridge, University Library Ff. 2. 38. A useful discussion of the language and provenance of the Northern *Octavian*, along with a consideration of the poem's relationship to both its probable source, and the Southern version of the romance, can be found in Frances McSparren's edition of the romance. See *Octavian*, pp. 21–52. McSparren has also edited the Southern version of the romance. See *Octavian Imperator*, ed. Frances McSparren, Middle English Texts 11 (Heidelberg: Universitätsverlag C. Winter, 1979).

to sail past the island on which her child and the lioness are living. She asks to be taken ashore to retrieve her son, and when she comes to the lioness's den, the animal ['thurgh Goddis grace' (463)] meekly allows her to reclaim the child. Then, accompanied by the lioness, and carrying the boy in her arms, the Empress returns to the ship and continues on her journey to the Holy Land. When she arrives in Jerusalem she is recognised by the King of that city, who invites her to join his household. There, living with the lioness, which has become her child's constant companion, she is treated with all the dignity that her royal status demands. Her son is christened Octavian, and in due course is made a knight by the King.

Having safely settled the Empress, her son, Octavian, and the lioness at the court of the King of Jerusalem, the romance turns to the fate of the second of the two children, whom as we have seen was carried off by an ape in the forest. And it is with the growth into manhood of this second child, and the gradual emergence of his true, noble identity, that the remainder of the romance is principally concerned. A whole series of extraordinarily improbable coincidences eventually results in the adoption of the child, who is named Florent, by a Parisian merchant and his wife, and he is raised completely oblivious of his true origins, believing himself to be their natural son. But although Florent is brought up almost from birth in the highly bourgeois milieu of urban Paris, his innately aristocratic nature prevents him from participating in middle-class life. The attempts of his adoptive parents to find him an occupation prove futile, as Florent displays a typically aristocratic disdain for money and trade. But while he is incapable of holding down a job, he finds himself irresistibly drawn to traditional aristocratic interests and pursuits such as falconry. When the Sultan of the Saracen kingdom besieges Paris, Florent's heroic exploits on the battlefield bring him to the attention not just of the King of France, but of his own father, who has come to Paris to help in its defence. Because neither monarch can believe that Florent is the child of a mere merchant, they summon the young man's adoptive father, and so discover that Florent is in fact Octavian's son. Octavian then rides out with his son and the King of France to do battle with the Sultan, but despite performing heroic deeds, the three men are taken prisoner. However, deliverance comes in the form of young Octavian, who has travelled to Paris along with his mother and the lioness to do battle with the Saracens. Such is his courage and valour – and with the lioness fighting ferociously by his side – that young Octavian vanquishes the Sultan and his army, and liberates his father and brother.

The family is then joyfully reunited and reconciled. Finally, discovering the treachery of his own mother, the Emperor resolves to have her burnt. But he is prevented from so doing when he hears the news, which is greeted with universal delight, that she has already killed herself by cutting her own throat.

Perhaps what is most immediately striking about *Octavian*, and that is evident even from this rather perfunctory summary of its plot, is the sheer romantic exuberance of the story. In typical romance fashion, nothing about the narrative is reserved or half-hearted. It is set in a marvellous, miraculous world where the normal laws of probability and cause and effect are swept aside with a lofty disdain. Its protagonists are conceived on a grand scale as models of virtue, nobility, heroism, and vice. It exhibits a moral and emotional confidence in its delineation of character and presentation of plot that a modern, more ironic sensibility would possibly regard as simplistic and naïve.

But when we turn aside from these more general, generic qualities, and concentrate instead on the representation of women in the narrative, something rather paradoxical emerges. For what we observe is that the principal female protagonist – the Empress – is presented as being both central and peripheral to the romance. So on one level, she can be seen as the focal point of the story: its moral and emotional centre. After all, she is the figure who both literally and figuratively follows the archetypal romance path of loss and restoration, and exile and return.[12] And yet although the Empress seems to occupy a place at the very heart of the narrative, there is at the same time an opposing tendency that has the effect of pushing her towards its margins. Significantly, the eponymous title of the romance suggests that it is the husband and not the wife who is the tale's dominant figure, an implication that is further reinforced by the tale's opening rubric: 'Here Bygynnes the Romance off Octovyane'. This sense of exclusion is further heightened when the Empress almost completely disappears from the second part of the romance, as the focus of the narrative dramatically shifts from her tale of suffering, loss, and exile, to the comically inflected story of Florent's growth into manhood and his gradual discovery of his true identity.[13] Added to this is the curious fact

---

[12] For an analysis of the structure of romance that pays particular attention to these archetypal patterns, see Northrop Frye, *The Secular Scripture: A Study of the Structure of Romance* (Cambridge, MA: Harvard University Press, 1976).

[13] In the Introduction to her edition of *Octavian* [p. 62], Frances McSparren notes that the so-called persecuted wife story 'has . . . been displaced from [its] central position in the poem'.

that the Empress's name is never revealed. Throughout, she is identified and defined exclusively in terms of her relationships with men. So while we are variously told that she is the daughter of the King of Calabria (190), the wife of the Roman Emperor, Octavian, and the mother of her two sons, there is a lingering sense that she is never fully regarded as a person in her own right.

Of course, to a contemporary audience, the anonymity of the Empress, if noticed at all, could have been viewed in a much more positive light as a sign of selflessness. In other words, it may have been interpreted as evidence of the Empress's willingness to live for others rather than for herself. And this self-sacrificing quality seems to be bound up in particular with her role as a mother. The Empress is presented as the personification of loving, patient, and self-sacrificing motherhood, and in this regard it is no coincidence that she is so insistently and persistently associated with the Virgin Mary. Thus, the Empress enlists the help of the Virgin Mary at the very opening of the narrative when praying with her husband for a child (73–84), she turns to the Virgin during what is perhaps her greatest moment of anguish, when she is about to be burnt with her children at the orders of her husband (261–7); and it is 'Thurgh þe myghte of Mary mylde' (466), that the Empress is able to tame the lioness, and retrieve her child from the animal's lair.

So through the Empress and her identification with the Virgin Mary the romance presents a whole complex of ideas and ideals that are conventionally associated with motherhood. But this Marian notion of the saintly, loving, suffering, and self-denying mother, embodied so perfectly by the Empress, meets its antithesis in the romance in the person of the Empress's wicked mother-in-law. For just as the Empress is presented as an unambiguous force for good, so her mother-in-law is irredeemably evil. After all, it is the mother-in-law who sets the whole course of events in motion by claiming that the Empress is an adulteress and that her two sons are illegitimate. She even goes so far as to provide her son with the ocular proof of his wife's guilt, by bribing 'a knaue' (124) to lie next to the Empress while she is sleeping. And perhaps what is most striking about the portrayal of Octavian's irreparably wicked mother is that no attempt is made to rationalise or account for her actions. She is simply evil, and as such she acts in an evil way.

This stark polarisation between the tale's two versions or manifestations of motherhood – the one the source of all good, the other the source of all ill – is, of course, a trope that is common to much

European folk literature, and that is extremely familiar to us today through such stock characters as the 'fairy godmother' and the 'wicked stepmother' of children's fairy tales. This division of the mother into two opposing figures seems to reflect an almost universal tendency in human cultural life, and it has given rise to a number of influential theories.[14] But while it is a phenomenon that is far from exclusive to the Middle Ages, it is certainly very characteristic of the era, and it acquires a peculiarly medieval resonance in *Octavian* through the Empress's association with the Virgin Mary.

While noting that motherhood tends to be treated ambivalently in medieval romance, Jennifer Fellows makes the further observation that the nature of the emotional response that it provokes is often determined by the degree to which the particular mother in question adopts either an active or passive role in the narrative. So according to Fellows: 'Broadly speaking, the more active the mother's part, at least in the initiation of events, the more likely she is to be in some degree the villain of the piece and eventually to meet with some sort of punishment or retribution.'[15] Fellows makes an important observation here; and one that applies particularly well to *Octavian*. For, as we have already seen, one of the qualities that identifies the Empress as a moral and virtuous character is her intense passivity, her silent and stoical acceptance of misfortune, and her complete refusal actively to resist it. Conversely, the Empress's mother-in-law is evil because she has a will of her own. Unlike the Empress, she actively intervenes in events in order to shape them for her own ends.

But although Fellows's model makes sense of the moral universe of *Octavian*, it works much less successfully when applied to the treatment of Olympias – the mother of Alexander the Great, and wife of King Philip of Macedon – in the fourteenth-century Middle English romance, *Kyng Alisaunder*. Olympias can in many ways be seen as a passive heroine who surrenders herself to the forces of destiny in much the same way as the Empress in *Octavian*. However, Olympias's destiny

---

[14] For an anthropological approach to the phenomenon, see Margaret Schlauch's classic study, *Chaucer's Constance and Accused Queens* (New York: AMS Press, 1927). Bruno Bettelheim offers a cogent account of the 'splitting' of the mother into good and bad figures in his highly regarded psychoanalytic interpretation of fairy tales. See Bruno Bettelheim, *The Uses of Enchantment: The Meaning and Importance of Fairy Tales* (New York: Knopf, 1977), pp. 66–73.
[15] Jennifer Fellows, 'Mothers in Middle English Romance', *Women and Literature in Britain, 1150–1550*, ed. by Carol M. Meale (Cambridge: Cambridge University Press, 1993), pp. 41–60 (at pp. 43–4).

is to give birth to the greatest hero the world has ever known, and this can only be accomplished, as we shall see, through an adulterous affair with a morally suspect man, who inveigles himself into her affections by claiming to be a god. Consequently, the portrayal of motherhood in *Kyng Alisaunder* has none of the moral clarity that we find in *Octavian*. There lingers a persistent sense of doubt and uncertainty about how to respond to Olympias: whether to condemn her as an adulteress, to laugh at her sexual antics and gullibility, or to revere her as the mother of the hero. Hence the romance tends to tie itself up in knots in its efforts to understand Olympias's moral character. And in an attempt to make sense of this morass of confused and conflicting emotions, I shall now turn to *Kyng Alisaunder's* treatment of the incident.

Kyng Alisaunder

The romance account of the conception of Alexander the Great is surely one of the most curious and puzzling episodes to be found in the canon of medieval literature, and its strange nature derives at least in part from its mingling of history with romantic legend. During the Middle Ages, knowledge of Alexander's life was principally derived from one ultimate source: a text that D. J. A. Ross has memorably described as: 'that strange mixture of inaccurately reported fact and fantastic fiction known to scholarship as *Pseudo-Callisthenes*'.[16] Composed in Greek by an unknown author some time between 200 BC and AD 200, and named after the historian Callisthenes to whom it is erroneously attributed in one of the manuscripts, *Pseudo-Callisthenes* has derivatives as far afield as Iceland, Ethiopia, and China, and was responsible for spreading Alexander's fame far beyond the borders of his historical empire.[17] A whole series of Latin translations of *Pseudo-Callisthenes* appeared throughout the Middle Ages, and it is from these Latin versions of the Greek text that the tremendously rich tradition of European vernacular literature about Alexander is derived, which includes the three surviving full-length treatments of Alexander's career in Middle English: *Kyng Alisaunder*, *The Wars of Alexander*, and *The Thornton Prose Life of Alexander*.[18]

[16] D. J. A. Ross, *Alexander Historiatus: A Guide to Medieval Illustrated Alexander Literature* (London: Warburg Institute, 1963).
[17] See Robin Lane Fox, *The Search for Alexander* (London: Little Brown, 1980), p. 40.
[18] See George Cary, *The Medieval Alexander*, ed. D. J. A. Ross (Cambridge:

In terms of its narrative function, the romance account of Alexander's miraculous conception can be seen to enhance his heroic credentials by providing him with a divine father from whom he can claim to have inherited superhuman powers. Similar incidents can be found in the legends of countless other heroes (such as Hercules), but what is remarkable in this case is that just such a desire for divine parentage possessed the historical Alexander. In the spring of 331 BC, after expelling the Persians from Egypt, Alexander travelled through the Sahara desert to the oracle of the Libyan god, Ammon (whom the Greeks identified with Zeus). According to the Greek historian, Arrian, Alexander 'had a feeling that in some way he was descended from Ammon . . . [and] he undertook this expedition with the deliberate purpose of obtaining more precise information on this subject'.[19] Alexander questioned the oracle in private, never making known what was revealed to him, but despite the secrecy that surrounded the incident it is reported that he was publicly greeted by the chief priest of the temple of Ammon, who is said to have addressed him as 'son of Zeus'.[20] The extent to which Alexander actually believed this claim to divine origins is a moot point, and one that not only provoked fierce controversy during his own lifetime, but that continued to elicit heated debate throughout the classical and medieval periods. However, from the point of view of the present discussion, the very fact that he made the claim is important because it is the ultimate source for the account of his conception that we find in both *Kyng Alisaunder*, and the wider romance tradition. Moreover, Alexander's claim to divine parentage

---

Cambridge University Press, 1956). For a study of the representation of Alexander in the British literature of the period, see Gerrit H. V. Bunt, *Alexander the Great in the Literature of Medieval Britain* (Groningen: Benjamins, 1994). All reference to *Kyng Alisaunder* will be to G. V. Smithers, ed., *Kyng Alisaunder*, Early English Text Society, Original Series 227, 237 (London: Oxford University Press, 1952–57).

[19] Arrian, *The Campaigns of Alexander*, Book 3, p. 151.

[20] According to Plutarch, the divine honour that the Libyan priest paid Alexander was in fact unintentional, resulting from his poor command of Greek: 'Others say that the priest, who wished as a mark of courtesy to address him with the Greek phrase "O, *paidion*" (O, my son) spoke the words because of his barbarian origin as "O, *pai dios*" (O, son of Zeus), and that Alexander was delighted at the slip of pronunciation, and hence the legend grew up that the god had addressed him as "O, son of Zeus".' See Plutarch, *Life of Alexander*, 27, trans. Ian Scott Kilvert, in *The Age of Alexander* (Harmondsworth: Penguin, 1973), pp. 283–4.

sealed the posthumous reputation of Olympias. For it introduced the story of her bizarre sexual encounter with Alexander's father, which seems to have irreparably tarnished her moral character in the eyes of medieval opinion.

However, although ultimately derived from Alexander himself, the romance account of his miraculous conception is further complicated by a local Egyptian legend that identified the Macedonian emperor as the son of the last indigenous Egyptian pharaoh, Nectanebo II.[21] A new narrative emerged from the combination of these two quite separate legends, and it is this composite account of Alexander's conception that came to be transmitted through *Pseudo-Callisthenes* to the romance tradition of the Middle Ages. Much of the confusion experienced by medieval authors when relating Alexander's conception can be put down to the fact that the story they related was formed almost by a process of compromise, as two quite distinct legendary traditions were forced together and merged. So before turning to *Kyng Alisaunder* and its representation of the narrative of Alexander's conception it will be helpful to have a sense of how that narrative came into being in the first place.[22]

Nectanebo II – the last indigenous pharaoh of Egypt, and the putative father of Alexander the Great – fled Egypt in 343 BC before the advancing armies of the Persian emperor, Artaxerxes III. But while it is now generally believed that he took refuge in Ethiopia (where he entirely vanishes from the historical record), an alternative destiny is ascribed to him by a nationalist Egyptian legend (which would seem to have been circulating as early as the third century BC), according to which he actually travelled to Macedonia where he became first the lover of Olympias, Philip's wife, and then in due course the father of Alexander, her son.[23] This legend therefore enabled the Egyptian people of the third century BC to claim Alexander as a native hero, and to view his invasion of their land

[21] The Egyptian background to the romance tale of Alexander's birth is explored by Betty Hill in her article: 'Alexander Romance: The Egyptian Connection', *Leeds Studies in English* 12 (1981), 185–94.
[22] I rely on Betty Hill's account ('Alexander Romance: The Egyptian Connection') for my discussion of this process.
[23] For the fate of Nectanebo, see Robin Lane Fox, *Alexander the Great* (London: Allen Lane, 1973), p. 197. In the introduction to his translation of *Pseudo-Callisthenes*, Richard Stoneman explores the Egyptian milieu from which the nationalist legends of Nectanebo and Alexander emerged. See Richard Stoneman, trans., *The Greek Alexander Romance* (Harmondsworth: Penguin, 1991), pp. 11–12.

not as yet another inglorious foreign conquest, but as a great patriotic victory over their hated enemies, the Persians.[24]

This Egyptian account of Alexander's conception, while seemingly incompatible with Alexander's own professed beliefs in his divine parentage, was in fact ingeniously combined with it to form the version of the story found in the romance tradition. The Libyan god, Ammon, provides the link between the two alternative accounts, for not only had he been appropriated by the Greeks, and identified with their god, Zeus, but he had also been assimilated by the Egyptians into their pantheon, and equated with the ram-headed god, Amun, the creator of the universe, and the divine father of the pharaoh.[25] It was Amun's role as the begetter of the pharaoh, a function that he performed by making love to the consort of the reigning monarch in the guise of her husband, that enabled these two seemingly incompatible legends to be reconciled.[26] For, once Alexander, who had assumed the title of pharaoh by right of conquest in the autumn of 332 BC, went on to identify himself as the son of Ammon at Siwah in 331 BC, it was possible for the Egyptian people to interpret these claims in the light of their own religious beliefs, and so assert that in accordance with the customary Egyptian practice, *their* god Amun had adopted the form of the pharaoh, Nectanebo, in order to conceive their future king, Alexander.

Thus, the account of Alexander's conception that finally found its way into the romances was composed of elements drawn from two seemingly incompatible sources. In this composite story, Alexander could be identified as the son of both Ammon and Nectanebo, although this somewhat complex resolution inevitably presented those medieval writers (such as the author of *Kyng Alisaunder*), who were faced with the task of making sense of the material, and who presumably possessed little knowledge of either ancient history or comparative religion, with considerable scope for confusion and misunderstanding.

---

[24] The author of *The Greek Alexander Romance* refers to this Egyptian legend at the very beginning of his work: 'Many say that he [Alexander] was the son of King Philip, but they are deceivers. This is untrue; he was not Philip's son, but the wisest of the Egyptians say that he was the son of Nectanebo, after the latter had fallen from his royal state.' See *The Greek Alexander Romance*, 1, 35.

[25] The absorption of Ammon into the system of Egyptian religious belief is discussed by H. W. Parke in *The Oracles of Zeus: Dodona-Olympia-Ammon* (Cambridge, MA: Harvard University Press, 1967), pp. 194–7, and by Fox, *Alexander the Great*, p. 202.

[26] See Betty Hill, 'Alexander Romance', pp. 185–6.

In *Kyng Alisaunder*, the historical Nectanebo is transformed into the mysterious figure of the Egyptian king, Neptenabus, a monarch wise in the arts of astrology and magic, who learns through the exercise of those arts that his land is soon to be conquered by an army led by Philip of Macedon. In order to avoid this impending defeat, Neptenabus flees his kingdom, and, determined to gain his revenge on Philip, he journeys to Macedoyne, Philip's capital, where Queen Olympias is reigning in her husband's absence. Overwhelmed by the Queen's physical beauty, Neptenabus manages to obtain a private audience by claiming to be a revered Egyptian astrologer. During their meeting he prophesies that she will soon be abandoned by Philip for a new wife, yet he is able to console her with the news that she will give birth to a son begotten by the god, Ammon, and that her child will grow up to avenge Philip and conquer the world.

That night, while Olympias is sleeping, Neptenabus casts magic spells over a waxen image of the Queen, causing her to have an extraordinary dream in which a dragon comes to her chamber, enters her bed, and impregnates her. The following morning, believing the dream to be a confirmation of Neptenabus's prophecy, and now entirely confident in the truthfulness of his testimony, Olympias invites him to become a member of her household, and entrusts him with all of her private affairs. That night, Neptenabus secretly disguises himself as Ammon by covering his body with dragon skin and concealing his face behind a mask of a ram's head, and in this guise he comes to Olympias's bed, where she conceives Alexander, her son.

Paradoxically, then, Neptenabus is revealed to be at one and the same time both a charlatan and a true prophet. Motivated by a mixture of lust and vengeance, he manages to trick his way into Olympias's bed by fabricating a fictitious story about the god, Ammon, and yet as a result of their adulterous union the Queen does indeed give birth to a remarkable son, just as Neptenabus prophesied. The magical dream that Neptenabus induces in the Queen is absolutely central to the deception that he practises on her, and, reflecting the ambiguous character of its author, the dream itself turns out to be both a misleading travesty, and a truthful prophecy, of future events:

> þe leuedy in her bed lay,
> Aboute myd-niȝth, ar þe day,
> Whiles he made his coniuryng,
> She seiȝ ferly in her metyng.
> Hire þouȝth a dragoun adoune liȝth

> To hire chaumbre and made a fliȝth.
> Jn he com to hire boure
> And crepe vnder her couertoure.
> Many siþe he hire kyste
> And fast in his armes þriste,
> And went away so dragon wylde;
> Ac gret he lete hir wiþ childe.   (lines 343–54)

A 'dragon wylde' (353) is indeed a suitably alien and awe-inspiring form for a divine being to adopt, for not only does it aptly suggest the otherness of a god's nature, but its appearance, like that of a god, is liable to instil in any human observer a profound sense of fear. Terror is certainly the overriding emotion experienced by Olympias on waking up – 'Olympias of slepe awook. / She was a-grised for þe nones, / þat alle quakeden hire bones' (356–8) – and in the dream itself it would seem that her extremely submissive response to the forceful, even violent approach of the domineering dragon is motivated by her fear of him. Whatever its pleasures and compensations, then, sex with a god, at least as depicted in Olympias's dream, would seem to be a profoundly shocking and frightening experience, and any child born of such an unnatural union, it is implied, would inevitably inherit some of the superhuman powers of its divine father. So it would appear that at this juncture the author's sympathies are with Olympias. For not only have we been told that her philandering husband, Philip, is about to leave her; but we have also observed the awe and terror she experiences on encountering what seems like a divine presence. Moreover, the whole episode is treated with a seriousness that borders on the reverential.

On the following night, Neptenabus attempts to reproduce Olympias's dream experience in reality by first changing his appearance to resemble that of a dragon, and then making love to the Queen in that guise:

> Jn bed wook dame Olympyas,
> And aspyed on vche manere
> ȝif she miȝth ouȝth yhere
> Hou Amon þe god shulde come.
> Neptenabus his charme haþ nome,
> And takeþ hym hames of dragoun,
> From his shuldre to hele adoun;
> His heued and his shuldres fram
> He diȝtteþ in fourme of a ram.
> Ouere hire bed twyes he lepeþ,

þe þrid tyme and jn he crepeþ.
Offe he cast his dragons hame
And wiþ þe lefdy playeþ his game.
She was þolemood and lay stille;
þe fals god dude al his wille.
Also ofte so he wolde,
þat game she refuse nolde.   (lines 380–96)

It has been suggested that the poet's treatment of this incident, with the emphasis on Neptenabus's deception and sexual exploitation of Olympias, owes more to the genre of fabliau than to romance.[27] The passage certainly has a low-comic tone, and it is immediately apparent that 'þe fals god' (394), Neptenabus, bears very little resemblance to the awesome figure of Olympias's dream. Indeed, far from transforming himself into a dragon, the exiled King merely assumes a vaguely dragon-like appearance by covering his body with dragon skin, and then leaping twice over the Queen's bed (presumably in imitation of a dragon's flight), before lying down beside her. Thus, Neptenabus is presented not as a powerful god, but as a lecherous trickster who is able to take advantage of the Queen's credulity in order to satisfy his lust.[28]

This shift in mood from the reverent to the comic inevitably reflects badly on Olympias, who seems to be stripped of the dignity and sympathy that she previously commanded. No longer the sacred vessel selected by a god to bear his heroic son, she becomes instead an object of sexual desire who is treated with contempt by the lustful man who deceives her. Moreover, although Neptenabus's disguise is woefully inadequate and unrealistic, the very fact that he is associated with animals might suggest that the kind of sexual gratification that he seeks is particularly grunting and animalistic in nature, an interpretation that would seem further to objectify and undermine Olympias. And it is not simply Neptenabus who fails to respect Olympias: the fabliau tone, with its explicit sexual detail – 'þe fals god dude al his wille / Also ofte so he wolde' – invites a voyeuristic and vicarious

---

[27] See Betty Hill, 'Alexander Romance', p. 189.

[28] Of course, as well as covering himself with dragon skin, which he removes once he gets into bed with the queen, Neptenabus also wears a mask of a ram's head, no doubt as a gesture towards the ram-headed Ammon. However, by combining both dragon and ram elements in his disguise, Neptenabus ends up resembling neither the dragon of Olympias's dream, nor the ram-headed god of Libyan tradition. In a sense, Neptenabus invests himself with too much significance, and his attempt to forge on to his one body two quite separate symbolic identities merely has the effect of exposing him still further as a fraud.

response from the implied reader, who in the case very definitely appears to be understood as male.

Conclusion

Despite their very obvious differences, it is nonetheless possible to detect certain underlying affinities in the treatment of women in *Octavian* and *Kyng Alisaunder*. For although the Empress in *Octavian* inspires respect and sympathy, while Olympias's predicament elicits laughter and derision, on reflection, the two texts are perhaps not as polarised as they might at first appear. In *Octavian*, although the Empress is viewed as the embodiment of everything that is good, she meets her equal but opposite in the form of her wicked mother-in-law, who is so irredeemably evil that her grisly suicide is not only presented as a cause for celebration and laughter, but is seen as a fittingly joyful event on which to conclude the romance. Thus, it would seem that at the same time as women are venerated through the Empress, they are denigrated through her mother-in-law. To adopt a rather modish phrase, the representation of the moral character of women in *Octavian* is a 'zero sum gain'. Moreover, the particular form of femininity that the romance idealises is the undemanding, self-denying kind that presents absolutely no challenge to masculine authority. Even when she is condemned along with her two children to be burnt to death for an act that she did not commit, the Empress meekly accepts her fate, and refuses to reproach her husband, whom the romance exonerates anyway by placing all the blame on his mother.

The emotional ambivalence that is evident in *Octavian* – but that is expressed through the two female characters – is focused singularly on the figure of Olympias in *Kyng Alisaunder*. Unlikely as it may at first appear, Olympias's predicament in various ways resembles that faced by the heroine of *Octavian*. As we have seen, when she is first introduced in the narrative, Olympias is about to be rejected by her husband, and this confers on her something of the victim status that is endured by the Empress. Moreover, like the Empress, Olympias is an entirely passive figure. Throughout her ordeal, she allows herself to be governed by what she considers to be, and what in many ways are, the dictates of a higher power. But through absolutely no fault of her own, Olympias finds herself facing a no-win situation. In order to obey the forces of fate or destiny that have chosen her to be the mother of Alexander, Olympias must first degrade herself – in the eyes of medieval opinion, at least – by submitting to a squalid sexual encounter with a seedy and deceitful man. So although, as previously suggested, much of the confusion generated by this episode derives from, and is inherent within, its source material, the treatment of Olympias nevertheless exposes the ambivalence and emotional uncertainty of medieval romance in its representation of women in general, and of their roles as wives and mothers in particular.

Rough Girls and Squeamish Boys: The Trouble with Absolon in The Miller's Tale[1]

GREG WALKER

ABSOLON, THE SQUEAMISH PARISH CLERK in Chaucer's *Miller's Tale*, is, perhaps, a predictable focus for an investigation of gender and genre in medieval literature. He has been the subject of considerable scholarly interest in the past two decades, and a variety of conflicting accounts have been offered of his sexuality, his attitudes towards women, and his literary origins. In part he remains a fruitful source of inspiration precisely because he is so difficult to pin down, both sexually and generically. But, as what follows will suggest, the attempt is worthwhile, both for what it implies about the gendered dynamics of humour in the *Tale*, and for its wider generic implications.

One of the purposes of this essay, as my subtitle suggests, is to examine just what is troubling for and about Chaucer's squeamish parish clerk. The trouble *for* Absolon, the apparently disproportionate horror he experiences when he kisses Alisoun's 'nether ye' (or perhaps, more accurately, when he reflects on the implications of that kiss immediately afterwards), is one part of the problem; and takes us into the world of psychoanalysis and gender theory. But the essay will also consider the trouble *with* Absolon, why it is that he troubles *us*; why he continues to provoke interest and discussion among scholars and readers of the *Tale*. Part of his troublesomeness, as I have suggested, lies in the way in which he defies categorisation, how he troubles the boundaries between male and female, masculine

[1] In the early part of this essay, I revisit material taken from an earlier essay, 'Laughable Men: Comic Stereotypes from Chaucer to Shakespeare', published in Roberta Mullini, ed., *Theta* VI (2002), pp. 1–16. I am grateful for the opportunity to reproduce some of that material here, and to the Leverhulme Trust, whose grant of a Major Research Fellowship gave me the time in which to work on this essay. I am also very grateful to my colleagues Drs Emma Parker, Anne Marie D'Arcy, and David Salter (now of the University of Edinburgh), and to Dr Claire Jowitt of the University of Wales, Aberystwyth, each of whom read earlier drafts of this essay and asked critical questions that helped me to rethink the implications of what I was trying to say.

and feminine, adult and child, and resists the easy binary oppositions so important to conventional ideas of identity. But he is also troublesome in generic terms, he crosses the boundaries and muddies the waters between fabliau, romance, moral exhortation and biblical narrative. He is, to borrow Mary Douglas's well-known formulation, 'matter out of place' and so an aberration, a problematic, liminal thing, as much between genres as he is between genders.[2] Hence it is fitting that his defining moment should involve a dangerous meeting of opposed categories of being in an archetypally liminal space, the bringing together of his 'pure' lips (wiped dry for the task) and a decidedly impure arse projected disruptively through the frame of a 'shot' window.[3]

Sexuality and the Somewhat Squeamish Male

Most accounts of Absolon have assumed that he is funny – and in one way or another inadequate – because of his inappropriate femininity.[4] This seems to me to be a problematic, or at least only partially satisfactory, claim. In what follows I will re-examine Absolon's character, and his role in The Miller's Tale, concluding rather that it is his adoption and internalisation of a fundamentally patriarchal (in a number of senses of the word) ideological stance regarding womanhood that makes him such a laughably inadequate figure in the world of the tale. His relationship – such as it is – with Alisoun, the carpenter's wife whom he pursues with gifts and love songs, is not informed by any

[2] Mary Douglas, Purity and Danger: An Analysis of Concepts of Pollution and Taboo (London: Routledge, 2000).
[3] I am grateful to Dr Emma Parker for suggesting to me the significance of the window as a frame for the famously 'misdirected' kiss.
[4] Anne Laskaya, Chaucer's Approach to Gender in the Canterbury Tales (Cambridge: D. S. Brewer, 1995), p. 87 ('Absolon is the only man in the tale who is described as feminine, and he is the man most maligned by the crude events of the tale'); Paul E. Beichner, 'Characterisation in The Miller's Tale', in Chaucer Criticism, Volume One: The Canterbury Tales, ed. by Richard Shoek and Jerome Taylor (Notre Dame, IN: University of Notre Dame Press, 1960), pp. 117–29 (at p. 119) ('Absolon . . . is too ladylike, and therein lies much of the humour when his fall occurs'); H. Marshal Leicester Jnr, 'Newer Currents in Psychoanalytical Criticism and the Difference "IT" Makes: Gender and Desire in The Miller's Tale', English Literary History 61 (1994), 473–99 (at p. 488) ('It has long been recognised that much of the satire in the portrayal of Absolon is constructed by feminizing him; here the man who acts too much like a woman is punished for both his gender and class treachery by having his feminization shoved in his face by a woman who acts like a man').

common 'feminine' traits or shared understanding. Nor is it directed by the conventional bodily urges of the fabliau male. As a result he quite literally does not know how to take her, with, as they say, hilarious consequences (for everyone but him). Yet, nor does the reader know how to take Absolon, hence the laughter that he evokes is at best awkward and at times frankly embarrassed. Is the humour of the kiss implicitly homophobic, or misogynist, or both? Do we laugh because we know that, in the same situation, we would behave in exactly the same way as Absolon does, or because we hope that we would not? The text does not provide ready answers to such questions. In this, I will argue, Chaucer is both exploring the conventions and implications of his chosen genre, and also tilting, if only obliquely, at a wider and more influential target.

Part of what makes Absolon memorable is, as many critics have pointed out, that he, like his kiss, is so obviously misplaced, grotesquely out of keeping with the prevailing tone and ethos of the tale that he inhabits. It is as if he had wandered into the fabliau from somewhere else, bringing the assumptions and behaviour patterns of that other world with him. In what follows I will explore this idea further, and suggest that this 'somewhere else' is not, as is sometimes argued, the world of romance, the most likely home for young men who court their beloveds with poetry and song, but the realm of popular religion, and in particular of the kind of religiosity that characterises aspects of the medieval drama. In finding Absolon's natural habitat in the religious cycle drama I am following a recent essay by Linda Lomperis that provided an important stimulus to my own thinking on the *Tale*, but I shall take the argument to rather different conclusions, and so hope-fully justify a further examination of some of the same issues.[5]

In Chaucer's *Miller's Tale*, as in fabliaux generally, sexuality is frankly acknowledged. Desire, satisfaction, and the pleasure to be gained from sexual activity are all taken as given facts of life. Hence the reader is assumed to be – indeed is constructed as – mature enough to understand and accept the nature of the pleasures that sex offers. Chaucer's description of the adulterous 'melodie' (MT, 3652)[6] that Nicholas the scholar and Alisoun enjoy together in John the carpen-ter's bed is thus not euphemistic but analytical, a reference to the

[5] Linda Lomperis, 'Bodies that Matter in the Court of Late Medieval England and in Chaucer's *Miller's Tale*', *Romanic Review* 86 (1995), 243–64.
[6] All references to Chaucer's writings refer to L. D. Benson, ed., *The Riverside Chaucer* (Oxford: Oxford University Press, 1987).

delightful nature of their 'bisynesse of myrthe and solas', rather than a coy refusal to name the deed.[7] It is only with the arrival of Absolon that the notion of taboo is introduced – manifestly belatedly and inappropriately – into the narrative. And with him comes a bowdlerisation of human experience and all its attendant baggage (chiefly the infantilisation of male sexuality and the neutralisation of female desire that it necessitates) which is drawn from a very different discourse and realm of experience.

Significantly, of course, Absolon arrives in the tale after the crucial, self-sufficient narrative of the Alisoun-Nicholas-John plot has been established and sent on its way to a denouement. And it is distinctive of Absolon's role to bring too little, too late to any situation to have any positive effect on events. If the classic relationship in both chivalric and fabliau competition is the erotic triangle, two men in pursuit of a single woman,[8] then Absolon is already geometrically excessive and surplus to requirements at his first arrival. It is John the carpenter whom Nicholas must defeat in order to enjoy Alisoun, not Absolon. And Alisoun has already responded affirmatively to Nicholas's proposition, signalling the first part of his victory over her husband prior to Absolon's appearance. Moreover, the lodger's shameless groping of Alisoun 'by the queynt' in the orchard (3275–6) has set the tale's linguistic and moral parameters at a level of frankness far beyond the tolerance of Absolon's coy, formal brand of courtship, long

---

[7] See, for example, the comments in Angela Carter, 'Alison's Giggle', originally published in *The Left and the Erotic*, ed. Eileen Phillips (London: Lawrence and Wishart, 1983), repr. in Angela Carter, *Shaking a Leg: Journalism and Writings*, ed. J. Uglow (London: Chatto and Windus, 1997), pp. 542–53. I am grateful to Emma Parker for bringing this essay to my attention, and to Nick Everett for tracking down a copy for me.

[8] This is, of course, the scenario that drives the *Tales* of the Knight, the Franklin, the Merchant, the Shipman, and the Squire, as well the Miller's offering, and it lies behind that of the Reeve. It is also the ostensible motor for the second half of *Sir Gawain and the Green Knight* and provides the core of the tragic movement in the Arthurian cycle in the relationship between Arthur, Guinevere, and Lancelot. For the notion of the erotic triangle, see René Girard, *Deceit, Desire and the Novel: Self and Other in Literary Structure*, trans. Yvonne Freccero (Baltimore: Johns Hopkins University Press, 1965), expanded and modified by Eve Kosofsky Sedgwick, *Between Men: English Literature and Male Homosocial Desire*, 2nd ed. (New York: Columbia University Press, 1992); and Martin Blum, 'Negotiating Masculinities: Erotic Triangles in the *Miller's Tale*', in *Masculinities in Chaucer: Approaches to Maleness in The Canterbury Tales and Troilus and Criseyde*, ed. by Peter G. Beidler, Chaucer Studies 25 (Cambridge: D. S. Brewer, 1998), pp. 37–52.

before the latter enters the scene with his desire for 'a kiss at least' (see 3680 and 3683). Consequently, Absolon's arrival does not for a moment threaten Nicholas's victory, albeit he does rather take the gloss off it (along with the skin from his arse) when he enacts his final, misdirected, revenge. Rather he presents a comic counter-case, reworking in a parodic key the courtship that Nicholas has already completed successfully in the authentic tones of fabliau comedy.

The iconography of Absolon's portrait has been sensitively analysed by Paul Beichner. Based upon the biblical Absalom, the son of David (II Samuel 14. 25–6), Absolon alludes to a number of exegetical themes. He is effete and luxuriant. His 'crull' golden hair, according to exegetical commentators, connoted excess,[9] and it, along with his skin, eyes, and fastidiously arranged clothes, are described in great detail in the manner of the *effectio*. The vocabulary deployed here, it is claimed, serves to feminise Absolon; but it also, more radically, infantilises him in images of smallness, prettiness, and inconsequentiality. Absolon's body is that of a child, and it is this that creates the main strand of humour in his portrait. His clothes are those of an infant dressed smartly for school, neat, prim, and in soft, unthreatening pastel colours. He is 'jolyf . . . and gay' (3339); with 'joly shode' (3316); is clad 'ful smal and proprely' (3320); his kyrtel is of 'lyght waget'; his surplice as white as blossom (3321 and 24). His movements are either small and precise or extravagant and ungainly (like his awkward, leggy dancing after the 'Oxford School' (3328–30)). His singing voice is a high soprano ('a loud quynyble' (3332)), later referred to as 'gentil and smal' like a warbling nightingale (3360), and it is no accident that his chosen musical instrument is a small rubible (3331) – a little fiddle – the very word for which sounds ungainly and silly. Taken together, these features serve to deny not simply his masculinity but his adulthood *per se*.[10] The final, seemingly gratuitous detail in his portrait, that 'he was somdeel squaymous / Of fartyng' (3337–8) – a generally admirable feature in a man, especially a parish clerk, but a grave handicap in the fundamentally visceral world of the fabliaux – 'and of speche dangerous' provides the final, broadest hint of his effete, bowdlerised nature.

That Absolon is feminine in appearance and manners is not necessarily a problem. Despite the claims of a number of critics to

[9] For Hugo of St Victor and Adam Scotus, Absalom's hair signified the excessive tendencies of human flesh and desire. See Paul E. Beichner CSC, 'Absolon's Hair', *Mediaeval Studies* 12 (1950), 222–33.
[10] Blum, 'Negotiating Masculinities', pp. 45–61.

the contrary,[11] femininity in a young man is a conventional feature of the successful heterosexual lovers of medieval literature. One need think only of Chaucer's Squire ('A lovyere and a lusty bacheler' (GP, 80), who none the less had 'lokkes crulle as they were leyd in presse' and wore clothes 'Embrouded . . . as it were a meede / Al ful of fresshe floures, whyte and reede' (81, 89–90)), or of Aurelius in The Franklin's Tale ('That fressher was and jollyer of array, / . . . than is the month of May' (FT, 927–8)) to substantiate the claim.[12] Even in fabliaux, the femininity of the hero is part of his lustiness, what marks him out as attractive to the women he pursues. Nicholas himself is 'lyk a mayden for to see' (3202), yet evidently has no difficulties in the role of heterosexual predator.

What is problematic, as we shall see, is not Absolon's femininity, but precisely his lack of access to female experience and his inability to empathise with the woman he pursues. He is narcissistic to the point of autism, incapable of entering even imaginatively into the thoughts, desires, or physical realities of anyone not conceived in his own image.[13] He insists upon abstracting Alisoun imaginatively from her bodily reality, displacing it where necessary into sanitised images of cats and mice, honeycomb, sweet cinnamon, small birds, and suckling lambs (3346–7; 3698–9, 3704). Whereas she is presented to us as a woman firmly grounded in the corporeal (her introduction tells us that

---

[11] See footnote 3, above.

[12] John Gower, in the Vox Clamantis (5, 225–40), complains that knights in love adopt womanish ways ('femineos mores'), but, again, this is presented as a heterosexual seduction device rather than a retreat from heterosexuality.

[13] See Laskaya, Chaucer's Approach to Gender, p. 86: 'His subjectivity blinds him to the possibility that Alisoun could have her own desires and wishes beyond, or in contradiction to, his own. He absolutely refuses to grant her autonomy; she is merely an extension of his own fantasy.' Kara Virginia Donaldson ('Alisoun's Language: Body, Text, and Glossing in Chaucer's "The Miller's Tale"', Philological Quarterly 71 (1992), 139–153), helpfully cites Hélène Cixous's essay 'The Laugh of the Medusa' (in E. Marks and I. de Courtivron, eds, New French Feminisms (Brighton: Harvester, 1985), pp. 245–64, at p. 251) to explain Absolon's deafness to Alisoun's voice. Cixous observes that, when a woman speaks, 'her words fall almost always upon the deaf male ear, which hears in language only that which speaks in the masculine'. But it is important to note that Absolon's 'deafness' goes beyond questions of gender. He is oblivious to debate – to speech of any kind – that is peripheral to his own immediate desires, hence his obliviousness to the jests of Gervays the smith as he awaits the coulter that will provide the instrument of his revenge. ('This Absolon ne roghte nat a bene / Of al his pley; no word agayn he yaf; / He hadde moore tow on his distaf' (3772–4)).

she scrubs her face hard to make it shine (3704), and plucks her
eyebrows (3310–11) – discreet signs of the intransigent bodily growth
that will become more obviously important later), he insists on denying
that corporeality. Hence, when the physical proof of the inadequacy of
his conception of femininity is brought home to him in a face full of her
'rough' pubic hair, he is entirely incapable of adjusting, and short-
circuits into violence. If Alisoun will not be as he imagined her, then
she must be entirely erased: only that will rectify the anomaly that she
presents and return his world to order.[14]

Absolon's pleasures, real and imagined, are, as a number of critics
have observed, entirely oral and visual.[15] His mouth itches in anticipation of kissing (3682); he dreams that he is at a feast (3684); describes
Alisoun, as we have seen, in terms of sweetmeats: honeycomb and sweet
cinnamon (3698–9); and longs for her like the lamb after the teat
(3704). He is indeed 'a myrie chylde', a toddler, whose pursuit of women
in general and Alisoun in particular is restricted to the voyeuristic
pleasures of observation from afar ('Sensyng the wyves of the parisshe
faste; /And many a lovely look on hem he caste, / And namely on this
carpenteris wyf. / To looke on hire hym thoughte a myrie lyf' (3341–4))
and the kind of indiscriminate gift-giving characteristic of the child in
Freud's anal stage, prior to entry into genital sexuality ('He sente hire
pyment, meeth, and spiced ale, / And wafres, pipyng hoot out of the
gleede; / And, for she was of town, he profred meede; / For som folk wol
ben wonnen for richesse, / And somme for strokes, and somme for
gentilesse' (3378–82)).[16] The narrator, entering into Absolon's thought
processes might speculate that:

> I dar wel seyn, if she hadde been a mous,
> And he a cat, he wolde hire hente anon.   (3346–7)

---

[14] Donaldson, 'Alisoun's Language', pp. 149–50.

[15] Laskaya, *Chaucer's Approach to Gender*, pp. 87–8; Peter Brown, *Chaucer at
Work: The Making of the Canterbury Tales* (London: Longman, 1994), p. 95. See
also Paul Strohm, *Social Chaucer* (Cambridge, MA: Harvard University Press,
1989), p. 135.

[16] Leicester, 'Newer Currents', p. 489, squares the circle between infantilisation and feminisation, suggesting that this kind of infantilism is itself encoded
as feminine: 'This disgusting, unmanly, and unrealistic condition is ordinarily
described as infantile, immature, pre-oedipal, and pre-genital, narcissistic,
masturbatory. Feminist psychoanalytic theory, however, has noted that this
kind of pleasure, after it grows up and goes through the Oedipus complex, is
also designated feminine, insofar as it is the pleasure of the castrated, what
women are stuck with.'

But, as Helen Phillips notes, it is only through such displacement that a satisfying consummation can even be imagined.[17] It is not merely 'if' but 'only if' the sexual act could be replaced by the more acceptably infantile satisfaction of eating that it would become thinkable for him. Given that she is not a mouse, nor he a cat, the relationship is doomed to go no further.

The building blocks of a potentially complex, even tragic, dysfunctional figure are all there, but the text keeps its exploration of Absolon resolutely within the comic register. The repeated use of 'joly' to describe his demeanour belies the potential seriousness of his 'woe', even before the text gets down to describing what 'courtship' really involves for Absolon (which, as V. A. Kolve suggests, seems to be merely frequent visits to the mirror and the dressing-up box):[18]

> From day to day this joly Absolon
> So woweth hire that hym is wo bigon,
> He waketh al the nyght and al the day;
> He kembeth his lokkes brode, and made hym gay;
> He woweth hire by meenes and brocage,
> And swoor he wolde been hir owene page;
> He syngeth, brokkyng as a nyghtyngale . . .
> Sometyme to shewe his lightnesse and maistyre,
> He pleyeth Herodes upon a scaffold hye.   (3371–7, 3383–4)

---

[17] Helen Phillips, *An Introduction to the Canterbury Tales: Reading, Fiction, Context* (Basingstoke: Macmillan, 2000), p. 57.
[18] V. A. Kolve, *Chaucer and the Imagery of Narrative: The First Five Canterbury Tales* (London: Edward Arnold, 1984), p. 187: 'For Absolon the process is its own reward, an excuse for dressing up, combing out his beautiful long hair, and waking while others sleep'; and p. 188, 'Whatever he may be up to, sexual desire seems at most tangential to it.' For similar views on Absolon's 'real' motivation, see Blum, 'Negotiating Masculinities', p. 44 ('Absolon makes his means his end . . . Instead of being a lover, he derives his satisfaction from impersonating one. There is even some doubt whether it is really a sexual union he is after, since it seems that a kiss is enough for him'), and pp. 45–6; Leicester, 'Newer Currents', p. 489: 'his pleasure . . . is derived from the skipping, "wynsing" activity of "paramours" itself; the acting and strutting and singing, and role-playing for their own self-consuming sakes, concealed and protected by the pretence of working to get the girl'. For the contrary view that Absolon is genuinely lecherous, see Laskaya, *Chaucer's Approach to Gender*, p. 91; D. Brewer, *A New Introduction to Chaucer*, 2nd ed. (London: Longman, 1988), p. 283; Wolfgang E. H. Rudat, 'The Misdirected Kisses in the *Miller's Tale*', *Journal of Evolutionary Psychology* 3 (1982), 103–8 (at p. 105); Peggy Knapp, *Chaucer and the Social Contest* (London: Routledge, 1990), p. 38.

But none of this succeeds since Alisoun's desires are already directed elsewhere. So the parish clerk is reduced to practising, metaphorically at least, another orally focused form of solitary pleasure,

> But what availeth hym as in this cas?
> She loveth so this hende Nicholas
> That Absolon may blowe the bukkes horn.   (3385–7)

Some Boys Do: Nicholas and Absolon

As we have seen, there are similarities between Nicholas and Absolon. Both are effeminate in manner, play musical instruments, and pursue Alisoun, each in his own way. But attempts to find equivalence between the two characters miss the point. They do similar things, certainly, and share a number of traits associated with the conventional roles and attitudes of the lover-seducer, but the similarities, such as they are, are merely superficial. Lomperis has, for example, noted the associations of each young man with fragrant herbs:

> Absolon is not so effeminate as to be unable to wield a phallic coulter, as he does at the tale's end, and Nicholas is not so masculine as to refrain from perfuming his room 'with herbes swoote' (3205), in the same manner as Absolon, who perfumes himself by chewing cardamom and licorice (3690). Early on in the narration, Nicholas himself is compared to licorice (3207). Both he and Absolon, it appears, are equally sweet-smelling.[19]

But the crucial distinction is, of course, that of authenticity. While Nicholas possesses a real penis and seems to employ it effectively, Absolon can only wield the artificial simulacrum of the phallus, the coulter, in a grotesque travesty of the procreative act. Here as elsewhere, Absolon's actions, while similar to those of Nicholas, are not performed 'in the same manner'; they are actions in bad faith. Nicholas smells as sweet as liquorice, whereas Absolon has to chew literal liquorice in a deliberate attempt (we are not told how successful) to achieve the same effect (3690–3). The same is true of their deployment of music and song. Nicholas strums his psaltery 'privelee' in his room, singing the *Angelus* in an attempt to lure Alisoun within, and plays an

---

[19] Lomperis, 'Bodies that Matter', p. 246. Kolve makes a similar comparison, Kolve, *Chaucer and the Imagery of Narrative*, pp. 165–6.

exuberant riff of triumph once she has agreed to his proposition. There is a direct and spontaneous relationship between music and desire. Absolon, conversely, plays his small rubible in the pubs and singles bars of Oxfordshire in an unfocused exhibition of public courtship: presenting himself to the ladies of the town, *en masse*, as a would-be amorous troubadour. In each case, the chewing of liquorice, the playing and singing, the dressing up as a gallant, these are actions that a man might play, part of a conscious performance, every bit as rehearsed and inauthentic as his (surely absurdly miscast) role as Herod on the scaffold high.

Absolon's vital role in the denouement of the tale is, like his introduction, carefully set up by the narrator as an exercise in both misjudgement of character and bathetic mis-timing. He re-enters the narrative in search of his kiss only after Nicholas and Alisoun have enjoyed their melodious night of sexual revelry, and his anticipation of the pleasures he might enjoy – again they are wholly oral in nature ('My mouth hath icched al this longe day; / That is a signe of kyssyng atte leeste. / Al nyght me mette eek I was at a feeste' (3682–4)) – seems again woefully adolescent when set against what has preceded them. There is thus a pleasing appropriateness to the form his humiliation is to take in the moment when the 'misdirected kiss' brings his lips into contact with Alisoun's arse and the world of the Bakhtinian 'lower bodily stratum':

> This Absolon down sette hym on his knees
> And seyde, 'I am lord at alle degrees;
> For after this I hope ther cometh moore.
> Lemman, thy grace, and sweete bryd, thyn oore'   (3723–6)
> This Absolon gan wype his mouth ful drie.
> Derk was the nyght as pich, or as the cole,
> And at the wyndow out she putte hir hole,
> And Absolon, hym fil ne bet ne wers
> But with his mouth he kiste hir naked ers
> Ful savourly, er he were war of this.
> Abak he stirte, and thoughte it was amys,
> For wel he wiste a womman hath no berd.
> He felte a thyng al rough and long yherd,
> And seyde, 'Fy! Alas! What have I do?'
> 'Tehee!', quod she, and clapte the wyndow to,
> And Absolon gooth forth a sory pas.   (3730–41)

That the clerk who had focused his expectations upon a sweet kiss should be paid for his trouble with one less saccharin is indeed apt. And the irony is not lost on the recipient. Nicholas's mocking 'A berd! A berd!' (3742) echoes Absolon's cry that the narrative does not provide at first hand:

> This sely Absolon herde every deel,
> And on his lippe he gan for anger byte,
> And to himself he seyde, 'I shal thee quyte'.   (3744–6)

But just why – and indeed how – is Absolon so effectively humiliated? As Linda Lomperis has observed, despite the text's apparent openness and abundance of anatomical detail ('hir hole' (3732), 'hir naked ers' (3734), 'a thyng al rough and long yherd' (3731)), there remains considerable scholarly disagreement about exactly where and upon what Absolon plants his lips. To Valerie Allen and Paul Strohm the description suggests Alisoun's anus, to Wolfgang Rudat her vagina. H. Marshall Leicester is engagingly disingenuous in weighing up the possibilities; 'it does not in fact sound like he has kissed an ass, but a cunt'.[20] The consensus seems to be that it must be either one thing or the other (only Lomperis bucks the trend and goes for the long-odds possibility that it is Alisoun's penis).[21] But, given that the night is as black as coal, and Absolon has sunk to his knees and is thrusting himself upwards with his eyes shut towards a body that is being squeezed out of a cramped shot-window, it is surely likely that he gets a face full of both at once. Thus the ritual indignity of the *osculum fundamentum* or *baise-cul* is combined with the parodic meeting of upper and nether lips in a carnivalesque act of uncrowning.[22] Additionally, given the (at best

---

[20] Valerie Allen, 'Blaunche on Top and Alisoun on Bottom', in *A Wyf Ther Was: Essays in Honour of Paule Mertens-Fonck*, ed. by Juliette Dor (Liege, 1992), pp. 23–9 (at p. 28); Strohm, *Social Chaucer*, p. 136; Rudat, 'Misdirected Kisses', pp. 103–8; Leicester, 'Newer Currents', p. 487.

[21] See Lomperis, 'Bodies that Matter', pp. 250–2 for the reasoning behind the striking claim.

[22] For the *baise-cul*, see M. Bakhtin, *Rabelais and His World*, trans. Helene Iswolsky (Bloomington, IN: Indiana University Press, 1984), pp. 373–7. It is interesting to note the terms employed in Bakhtin's description of 'uncrowning comedy' in *The Dialogic Imagination*: 'Laughter has the remarkable power of making an object come up close, of drawing it into a zone of crude contact where one can finger it familiarly on all sides . . . lay it bare and expose it freely and experiment with it. Laughter demolishes fear and piety before an object . . . This is the zone of maximally familiar and crude contact . . . Basically this is

basic) lavatorial hygiene of the period, there may also be in play here at least a hint of that fascination with kissing or eating shit evident in both the colloquial insult 'a turd in your teeth' and fabliaux such as *La Coille Noire* and *Le Débat du Con et du Cul*.[23]

Whether it is single, double, or triple, however, the insult to Absolon and the humiliation that it imparts are apparently devastating. His complete horror at the physicality of the encounter is reflected in the frenzied lengths to which he goes to remove any trace of Alisoun's savour from his all too sullied flesh:

> Who rubbeth now, who froteth now his lippes,
> With dust, with sond, with straw, with clooth, with chippes,
> But Absolon, that seith ful ofte, 'Alas!'   (3747–9)

This is no temporary embarrassment, but the end of his sexual ambitions for life:

> 'Allas', quod he, 'allas, I ne hadde ybleynt!'
> His hoote love was coold and al yqueynt;
> For fro that tyme that he dadde kist hir ers,
> Of paramours he sette nat a kers,
> For he was heeled of his maladie.
> Ful ofte paramours he gan deffie,
> And weep as dooth a child that is ybete.   (3753–9)

uncrowning, that is, the removal of an object from the distanced plane . . . In this plane (the plane of laughter) . . . the back and rear portion of an object (and also its innards not normally accessible for viewing) assume a special importance' (M. M. Bakhtin, *The Dialogic Imagination*, ed. by Michael Holquist, trans. by Caryl Emerson and Michael Holquist (Austin, Texas: University of Texas Press, 1981), pp. 23–4.) In his encounter with Alisoun's arse, Absolon is granted the opportunity to enter this world of uncrowning laughter, to replace his sterile, squeamish idealisation of both 'woman' as object and himself as subject with a liberating exposure to the realities of 'the lower bodily stratum'. However, rather than embracing the 'crude contact' and joining in the laughter, he recoils from it back to the safety of the 'distanced plane' from which he came – leaving himself the butt (so to speak) of Alisoun and Nicholas's laughter.

[23] For an excellent account of such tales, see Miranda Griffin, 'Dirty Stories: Abjection in the Fabliaux', in David Lawton, Wendy Scase, and Rita Copeland, eds, *New Medieval Literatures* III (1999), pp. 229–60. See also Laura Kendrick, *Chaucerian Play: Comedy and Control in the Canterbury Tales* (Berkeley, CA: University of California Press, 1988), p. 81; and Sarah M. White, 'Sexual Language and Human Conflict in the Old French Fabliaux', *Comparative Studies in Society and History* 24 (1982), 185–210.

Despite the text's having set us up – through reference to Absolon's particular brand of squeamishness – to expect his final quietus to be flatulent, his real humiliation is thus delivered here in the kiss. The fart that Nicholas ultimately bestows upon him is, however impressive in its dimensions and results ('As greet as it had been a thonder-dent, / That with the strook he was almoost yblent' – although it is not finally clear whether it is Nicholas that is nearly blinded by the effort, or Absolon by the blast), no more than an afterthought. Absolon has already discovered in the kiss a fundamental truth far more unsettling than the bodily function of which he had hitherto been so 'squaymous'.

What, then, are we to make of Absolon's frenzied reaction to what Rudat has memorably described as his 'involuntary act of (almost) cunnilingus'?[24] As Leicester has suggested, there seem to be clear echoes here of the primal scene imagined in Freud's late essay 'The Medusa's Head':

> The terror of the Medusa is . . . a terror of castration that is linked to the sight of something. Numerous analyses have made us familiar with the occasion for this; it occurs when a boy, who has hitherto been unwilling to believe in the threat of castration, catches sight of the female genitals, probably those of an adult, surrounded by hair, and essentially those of his mother.[25]

So it is tempting to see Absolon's kiss as re-enacting the moment when all toddlers discover 'the truth' about sexual difference at first hand, and hence to see Alisoun's thrusting of her arse out of the window as a defiant rejection of both Absolon's inept courtship and his sexual naïveté. For, as Freud goes on to say, the exposure of one's own genitals (especially if one is female) is an archetypal act of defiance:

> displaying the genitals is familiar in other connections as an apotropaic act. What arouses horror in oneself will produce the same effect upon the enemy . . . We read in Rabelais of how the Devil took to flight when the woman showed him her vulva.[26]

Still more powerfully, the kiss evokes Julia Kristeva's notion of the abject, with Absolon's horror echoing the reaction against the fluid

---

[24] Rudat, 'Misdirected Kisses', p. 105.
[25] Sigmund Freud, 'The Medusa's Head' (1922), cited in Leicester, 'Newer Currents', pp. 473–4.
[26] Leicester, 'Newer Currents', p. 474.

signs of sexual difference, the 'substances that cross bodily boundaries, that traverse physical thresholds' central to notions of abjection.[27]

But, if in psychoanalytic terms the kiss re-enacts yet another version of the primal encounter with female sexuality and its attendant castration anxieties (and in this respect it is interesting that at the moment that he initiates his revenge, his thoughts turn to his mother and her generosity ('Of gold', quod he, 'I have thee broght a ryng. / My mooder yaf it me, so God me save,' (3794–5)), in the public sphere it seems also to evoke the Bakhtinian notion of the clash between the grotesque and classical bodies. Again, to point this out is to say nothing new; but it is important to remember that these two readings are not alternatives – still less are they mutually exclusive. Freud and Bakhtin are telling essentially the same story, and Absolon's response to his encounter with Alisoun's arse neatly embodies the fact.

It has been objected against Bakhtin that his account of the classical and grotesque bodies neglects the crucial issue of gender;[28] but on closer inspection gender proves to be central (albeit tacit) to the opposition between the two bodies he describes (representing respect- ively the values of the clerical elite and the popular marketplace). The grotesque body, it will be remembered, is characteristically 'unfinished, [it] outgrows itself, transgresses its own limits', revealing 'an openness to the world'.[29] This seems a particularly apt delineation of Alisoun's 'rough and long yherd' 'hole', which is presumably also distended and fluid (both 'open' and 'transgressive') after her long night of merriment. It may be that Absolon's hair suggested excess to exegetically-inclined readers, but *his* hair is carefully combed and crimped. It is rather

---

[27] Julia Kristeva, *Powers of Horror: An Essay on Abjection*, trans. Leon S. Roudiez (New York: Columbia University Press, 1982), especially pp. 4 and 93–100. Kristeva's suggestion that a subject's existence in the symbolic order depends on 'a clean and proper body', that is one that rejects any of the 'improper, unclean and disorderly elements of corporeality', would seem very pertinent to Absolon's reaction to his kiss. The aptness of Kristeva's work for an understanding of Absolon's role in the *Tale* was brought to my attention by Dr Emma Parker. I am very grateful for the chance to discuss the idea of abjection with her, and to benefit from the succinct account of Kristeva's ideas in her essay, 'From House to Home: A Kristevan reading of Michèle Roberts's *Daughters of the House*', *Critique* 41 (2000), 153–73, from which I quote in the summary, above.
[28] See, for example, Gail Kern Paster, *The Body Embarrassed: Drama and the Disciplines of Shame in Early Modern England* (Ithaca, New York: Cornell University Press, 1993), p. 16.
[29] Bakhtin, *Rabelais and His World*, pp. 19, 25, 26.

Alisoun's unkempt pubic hair that represents the uninhibited indulgence in the bodily life of the world.

Such features as Bakhtin describes were, in terms of the classical medical theory that lies at the heart of medieval notions of physiognomy, characteristic of the female body. As Mary Harlow has recently demonstrated, the Hippocratic texts of the fifth and fourth centuries BC drew crucial distinctions between the male and female bodies in terms of their porousness and 'openness to the world'. According to this model,

> male bodies are dry and closed, while female bodies are spongier and more open, because of the nature of female flesh and the functions of the female body . . . indeed the open body, opened by menstruation, sexual penetration, and childbirth, is an inherently healthy female body, according to the Hippocratic corpus.[30]

Hence, as Harlow points out, the process by which women might find approval within the ascetic religious ideology of the clerical elite, involved explicitly 'becoming male' in both intellectual and bodily terms:

> The physical hardships and strict fasting that were practised by certain female ascetics might even produce a body that approached near to the masculine model of dry and closed. Lack of food could dry out the porous flesh of the female: it could even result in the suppression of menstruation, a defining female trait.[31]

It goes without saying that such a process also marked a movement in Bakhtinian terms from the grotesque body of the marketplace to the classical body of the church. What it might involve is graphically described in a letter of Basil of Caesarea (although here, as the final sentence quoted makes clear, the recipient is male):

---

[30] Mary Harlow, 'In the Name of the Father: Procreation, Paternity, and Patriarchy', in *Thinking Men: Masculinity and Self-Representation in the Classical Tradition*, ed. by Lyn Foxhall and John Salmon (London: Routledge, 1998), pp. 155–69. I am greatly indebted in what follows in this section to Harlow's essay, and the essay by Gillian Clark, 'The Old Adam: The Father and the Unmaking of Masculinity', pp. 170–82 in the same collection. I am grateful to my colleague Dr Felicity Rosslyn for bringing this volume to my attention. See also Joyce E. Salisbury, 'Gendered Sexuality', in *Handbook of Medieval Sexuality*, ed. by Vern L. Bullough and James A. Brundage (New York: Garland, 1996), pp. 81–102.

[31] Harlow, 'Name of the Father', p. 167.

Piercing your body with rough sackcloth, and binding your loins with a stiff belt, you resolutely put pressure on your bones. Through your abstinence, your sides become hollow . . . You collapsed your flanks from within like a gourd, forcing them to adhere to the area of your kidneys. Then, emptying your flesh of fat, you nobly dried out the channels of the hypogastric region, and by fasting compressed your stomach itself, so that you made your ribs, like the eaves of a house, cast a shadow over the place of your navel. So with your whole body shrunken, you confessed God's glory in the night hours, and with streams of your tears you soaked and smoothed your beard.[32]

The grotesque body, as described by Bakhtin, is, then, also the female body as imagined by medieval medical theory – and more generally the body that medieval thinking posited as 'feminine'. For it is only at those moments of openness, the 'shameful' moments of overindulgent eating, defecating, pissing, ejaculating, or being penetrated as a passive sexual partner, that the male body abandons its classical integrity and enters into the carnivalesque sphere of the grotesque.[33] In celebrating the openness, fluidity, and incompleteness of the grotesque body, as against the closed, dry body of the classical ideal, Bakhtin is reversing the traditional hierarchy of gender under patriarchy every bit as much as he is reversing the traditional social and cultural hierarchies of elite and plebeian, church and marketplace.[34]

To return to the primal scene of *The Miller's Tale*, what are we to make of poor Absolon and his horror? In almost all cases the critical assumption has been, curiously, that the text aligns itself with Absolon's repulsion at the corporeal, 'rough yherd' materiality of Alisoun's body. His realisation that such things are not really what he was looking for in life is taken to provide the moral of the tale – or at least of his part in it. It is the salutary experience that restores him to a more 'normal' perspective on life. As Anne Laskaya put it, 'Absolon's kiss forces his recognition of truth, his recognition of his own ridiculous delusions.'[35] But this seems an

---

[32] Basil of Caesarea, *Letter 45*, ed. Y. Courtonne, cited in Clark, 'Old Adam', p. 178.

[33] Bakhtin, *Rabelais and His World*, p. 26.

[34] See, for example, Bakhtin, *Rabelais and His World*, pp. 240–4: 'In this tradition woman is essentially related to the material bodily lower stratum; she is the incarnation of this stratum that degrades and regenerates simultaneously.'

[35] Laskaya, *Chaucer's Approach to Gender*, p. 87 ('He is rudely awakened to the "naked" truth about Alisoun, for no lady would bare her bottom to her lover in such a manner'), and p. 88 ('To be healed of his effeminacy, Absolon must be

overly generous interpretation of Absolon's response. It is hard to see any evidence in his subsequent near-hysterical behaviour of a recognition of any new truth about himself, or of an abandonment of his delusions. It is his view of Alisoun that changes as a result of the kiss, not his degree of self-awareness, and he simply shifts from one inherently misogynistic delusion (woman as incorporeal ideal) to another more overtly misogynistic one (woman as grotesque carnality).[36]

Even those consciously perverse readings that have tried to reverse the dynamic and celebrate, as it were, the cunt and not the kisser have seen themselves as reading against the grain to reveal a carnivalesque unconscious at work in the text that the narrator does not openly acknowledge. The assumption seems to be that the tale, being a work of elite culture, could not really be so openly subversive as to side with the grotesque body against its clerical critic and 'gloser'. But this implies too rigid a distinction between the elite and the carnivalesque. The kind of culture that Chaucer inhabited, poised between the city of London and the court, was itself porous and accommodating enough to embrace the grotesque body and all its implications. What we know of the royal court, its texts and ceremonies suggests very clearly that it too was not squeamish, but was happy to include the grotesque among its holiday entertainments (the most obvious example of which being the game of 'fart-prick-in-cul' included in Henry Medwall's *Fulgens and Lucres* for the entertainment of Archbishop Morton's household). In such an environment Absolon's fastidiousness would appear as ridiculous as it would in any other forum.[37]

aggressive. If he was love-sick before, he is "cured" at the end'). For similar approaches to the issue, see Kolve, *Chaucer and the Imagery of Narrative*, p. 193 (the kiss is 'the lesson this young parish clerk most needs to learn'), and p. 197 ('The hairy kiss restores him to his proper person, ending the make-believe and role-playing, breaking the game'); Allen, 'Blaunche on Top', p. 28 ('when she exposes her naked bottom she reveals the ugly essential nature beneath her skirt and completes the *descriptio* with its absent *notatio*'); Strohm, *Social Chaucer*, p. 136 ('The idealistic Absolon learns fast after his confrontation with Alisoun's hairy ass'). The most overtly 'normative' reading is probably Alan Renoir's, 'Absolon's reaction . . . is a piece of superb psychological realism, and any man who thinks he would react differently ought to make an emergency appointment with his analyst.' Alain Renoir, 'The Inept Lover and the Reluctant Mistress: Remarks on Sexual Inefficiency in Medieval Literature', in *Chaucerian Problems and Perspectives: Essays Presented to Paul E. Beichner*, ed. by Edward Vasta and Zacharias P. Thundy (Notre Dame, IN: University of Notre Dame Press, 1979), pp. 180–206 (at p. 201).

[36] See Donaldson, 'Alisoun's Language', p. 149.

[37] For the heterogeneity of late-medieval court culture, see Greg Walker, 'John

That the reader's response to Absolon's 'cure' is supposed to be as derisory as that toward his original malady is implied in the narrative itself, for in neither state is he aligned to the world-view of the tale. His self-mortification and abjuration of all 'paramours' are as absurd as was his earlier inept pursuit of the Oxford women with small rubible in hand. Significantly Absolon, like Malvolio in the finale of *Twelfth Night*, is entirely excluded from the cruel, cleansing communal laughter at John's expense that closes the tale, and which the narrator invites his audience to share. Unlike Malvolio, however, Absolon does not threaten through his exclusion to upstage the other characters and disrupt the sense of closure that the scene achieves. The world of *The Miller's Tale* closes ranks to mark his alienation as mockable, and consequently, as he frets at his lips and threatens vengeance, his case has none of the moral power that Malvolio achieves as he staggers from the dark house to declare that he has been done 'notorious wrong'.[38] Were the reader being encouraged to see Absolon's newfound asceticism as an admirable recovery of a true spiritual perspective after a period of worldly blindness (as some readings have suggested), his resolution would surely have been cast in a more plausibly moral or spiritual framework. As it is, it appears to be manifested simply in gratuitous self-mutilation and murderous, misogynist violence. All in all, the idea that Absolon is converted to a clearer sense of his spiritual duties by his experience seems unlikely. God might speak directly to sinners in a voice of thunder from the pages of the Bible, from clouds, even (we might note) on one occasion from within a bush, but there is no tradition of his doing so from an arse and in the form of a blinding fart.

Boys' Own Stories? Absolon, Squeamishness, and Romance

But, if Absolon is, and remains, laughable, what is it exactly that we are being invited to laugh at? Does the comedy have a wider reference than merely evoking a comic stereotype of certain kinds of male behaviour? One conventional answer to this question points towards

Skelton and the Royal Court', in *Vernacular Literature and Current Affairs in the Early Sixteenth Century: France, England, and Scotland*, ed. by Jennifer and Richard Britnell (Aldershot: Ashgate Press, 2000), pp. 1–16. For *Fulgens and Lucres*, Walker, ed., *Medieval Drama: An Anthology* (Oxford: Blackwell, 2000).
[38] *Twelfth Night*, V.1.324–75, in Stanley Wells and Gary Taylor, eds, *The Oxford Shakespeare: The Complete Works* (Oxford: Oxford University Press, 1999).

the rival literary genre of romance, claiming that the characterisation of Absolon is a deliberate mocking of the chivalric hero, part of the Miller's attempt to 'quite' *The Knight's Tale* and parody its values.[39] In this respect Absolon is read as a parodic version of Palamon and Arcite, and of the heroes of romance in general, and his inclusion in *The Miller's Tale* seen as a further gambit in Chaucer's ongoing fascination with the blurring and reworking of conventional literary genres.

Yet, is it true to say that Absolon brings the mood and ethos of courtly romance with him into the fabliau? He reproduces a number of the tropes of romance courtship, certainly; but he does so in a manner that falsifies the integrity of the genuine romance every bit as much as it fails to find the authentic note of the fabliau. His courtship of Alisoun has about as much in common with authentic courtly behaviour as the lies spun by Nicholas to deceive John have with the prophetic tradition of the Old Testament. Absolon is a creature of nurture rather than nature, self-fashioned (and that badly) in the image of the courtly lover; but crucially he is a failure, an amatory equivalent of the *miles gloriosus*. His behaviour would be as out of place and risible in a romance as it is in a fabliau.

The true romance sensibility is not infantilised – inhibited from growth and development as Absolon is – but more properly child-*like* in its approach to sexuality and sexual relations. Its innocence is not enforced but organic, a stage through which the central hero will pass in the quest for experience and self-knowledge. The chivalric hero is thus frequently a 'childe' only in the sense that he is a young man, inexperienced and questing, he is neither too young nor too ill equipped to deal with the challenges of adulthood when they arise. As Derek Brewer shrewdly observes, the typical romance 'is a story about being young, *and growing up*'.[40]

---

[39] See, for example, Lomperis, 'Bodies that Matter', p. 249; Leicester, 'Newer Currents', p. 482; Elisabeth Brewer, *Geoffrey Chaucer: The Miller's Tale* (Harlow: Longman, 1982), p. 38 ('Absolon is . . . a parody of the noble lover of romance'); Lee Patterson, '"No Man His Reson Herde": Peasant Consciousness, Chaucer's Miller, and the Structure of the *Canterbury Tales*', in *Literary Practice and Social Change in Britain, 1380–1530*, ed. by L. Patterson (Berkeley: University of California Press, 1990), pp. 113–55, pp. 131–2. But, as Derek Pearsall has argued, Absolon's 'love-talkyng' is so 'intrinsically ridiculous' 'that the joke is surely on him, and not on the courtly idealism of love that [he] get[s] so idiotically wrong'. Derek Pearsall, *The Canterbury Tales* (London: Everyman, 1985), p. 176.

[40] Derek Brewer, *Symbolic Stories: Traditional Narrative and the Family Drama in*

The sexual experiences of heroes such as Palamon and Arcite in Chaucer's *Knight's Tale*, or Gawain in *Sir Gawain and the Green Knight*, are presented as awkward and fraught with difficulty, but they are not ridiculous, whereas Absolon's behaviour is ridiculous in its own terms, regardless of the fabliau setting that renders it doubly risible. The world of romance, while it celebrates the courtliness and finer sensibilities of its ideal protagonists, is not squeamish about the body or its functions. As Patricia Ingham notes, the reader is not shielded from the gruesome physicality of Arcite's death in *The Knight's Tale*.[41] The knights of romance are not distanced or alienated from their own bodies, or from those of their allies and adversaries. They bleed copiously, they slice off giants' testicles, and clutch at their own intestines as they threaten to spill upon the ground. The romance world is thus a fundamentally visceral one, posited upon the fact of the common corporeality of humanity, even as it seeks to find distinctions among its inhabitants between the refined and the coarse, the noble and the base.[42]

English Literature (Cambridge: D. S. Brewer, 1980), p. 74, my italics. See also Susan Crane, *Gender in Middle English Romance* (Princeton: Princeton University Press, 1994), esp. p. 186. Northrop Frye also talked of 'the perennially child-like quality of romance' (Northrop Frye, *Anatomy of Criticism: Four Essays* (Princeton: Princeton University Press, 1971), p. 186ff.).

[41] Patricia Clare Ingham, 'Homosociality and Creative Masculinity in the *Knight's Tale*', in *Masculinities in Chaucer*, ed. by P. G. Beidler (Cambridge: D. S. Brewer, 1998), pp. 23–35, pp. 26–7.

[42] There are, of course, sub-genres of romance that do not focus openly on the visceral nature of human existence, and the corporeal consequences of martial endeavour. Such texts focus on the courtly and emotional aspects of the knightly experience, on deeds of love rather than of arms. *Sir Gawain and the Green Knight* dispenses with the whole business of combat in a single stanza (albeit the impending violence at the heart of Gawain's quest is displaced throughout the narrative in a powerful undercurrent of violence, most obvious in the hunting segments of Fitt Three), while the Breton Lay is generically inclined to focus away from the field of combat, as Chaucer's forays into the genre suggest. What Arveragus does to win honour in England in *The Franklin's Tale* is not investigated, and the knight of *The Wife of Bath's Tale*'s only act of violence is his violation of the young maiden at the start of the tale. But such tales are simply not interested in the visceral nature of bodily desire and its satisfaction. *The Miller's Tale* is different. It is very interested in that visceral quality, but has a central figure, in Absolon, who is incapable of recognising and responding to it. A helpful contrast is provided by Aurelius in *The Franklin's Tale*. Like Absolon, he expresses his courtly identity through singing and dancing in the company of women and a good deal of his description is taken up with accounts of his music-making. His sphere of operation is the private, household realm of love and dalliance rather than the public world of chivalric competition and deeds of arms. But, like Chaucer's Squire in the

If we look at some specific examples, beginning with Chaucer's own *Knight's Tale*, the point becomes clearer. In Chaucer's *Tale* Palamon and Arcite's desire for Emily is childlike, even childish in its competitive aspect, and immature in every sense, but it is manifestly genuine, prompted by and expressed through powerful and compelling emotional energies. The knights' desire for Emelye at first sight is represented as comic (hence the images used to describe it – buckets in a well, two dogs fighting over a bone – and the generally petulant tone in which it is discussed) but it is desire nonetheless. Both the powerful, urgent nature of Palamon's attraction to her and the possibility of its reciprocation (despite Emelye's long ignorance of his feelings and her initial unwillingness to wed) are hinted at in the mirrored responses of the two young aristocrats to the procreative stimulus of that first May morning. Both Emelye and Palamon occupy symbolic spaces suggestive of detachment from the natural and the bodily spheres. She, protected from the wilds beyond the city in her walled sanctuary of tamed vegetation (itself a tiny sanctuary within the walls of the wider city), and he, elevated above the base multitude in the lofty tower with its panoramic view of 'al the nobel citee', ought to be well placed, symbolically as well as geographically, to withstand the lures of base nature. But, as the text reveals, each is responding instinctively to the calls of May, the conventional metaphor for the urges of burgeoning sexual desire.

V. A. Kolve has drawn attention to the way in which these passages are structured around variations on the word 'roam', drawing tacit analogies between the two characters whose experience seems on the surface so different.[43] Palamon

> Was risen and romed in a chambre an heigh,
> In which he al the noble citee seigh,
> And eek the gardyn, ful of braunches grene,
> There as this fresshe Emelye the shene
> Was in hire walk, and romed up and doun.   (1065–9)

And it is important to appreciate the sexual charge that this 'roaming' has here, and its implications for the narrative. On a conscious level Emelye may be ignorant of Palamon and his feelings, but subconsciously she is responding to the same drives and urges, sublimating

---

General Prologue, and unlike Absolon, his character is founded upon a secure knowledge of the bodily realities of the world he inhabits.

[43] Kolve, *Chaucer and the Imagery of Narrative*, pp. 86–9.

them into the private rituals of 'Maying' which also serve to display her
availability as a sexual partner – a possibility reinforced by reference to
the physical proximity of their respective enclosures:

> The grete tour, that was so thikke and strong
> Which of the castel was the chief dongeoun,
> (Ther as the knyghtes weren in prisoun
> Of which I tolde yow and tellen shal)
> Was evene joynant to the gardyn wal
> Ther as this Emelye hadde hir pleyynge   (1056–61)

Each of them paces frustratedly back and forth within the confines of
their own enclosed spaces in a movement that tacitly bespeaks powerful unrequited and unacknowledged desires. The walled garden might
be a conventional symbol of all kinds of abstractions and retreats from
bodily nature (of prelapsarian perfection, the enclosed purity of female
virginity, of private reflection, and the wildness of nature tamed to
civility and order), but Emelye's actions within this particular garden
suggest that the unruly impulses of human sexuality reach even here.
Palamon paces impatiently in his high cell, placed in the head of the
hard, phallic tower, while Emelye traces a similar course, roaming up
and down in the fertile glade of the moist vegetative garden that
adjoins it:

> Er it were day, as was hir wone to do,
> She was arisen and al redy dight;
> For May wole have no slogardlie a-nyght.
> The sesoun priketh every gentil herte,
> And maketh hym out of his slep to sterte.   (1040–4)

> . . . in the gardyn, at the sonne upriste,
> She walketh up and doun, and as hire liste
> She gadereth floures . . .   (1051–3)

Nor does the poem disguise the painful realities of mature sexuality.
Diana (the goddess of childbirth as well as chastity, whose unwillingness to aid the woman at her feet crying out in the travails of labour
provides one of the most unsettling images of the highly disturbing
third part of the poem) offers Emelye a brutally honest appraisal of her
future prospects. The delayed extinguishing of one of the fires on the
altar and the subsequent oozing of blood from the rushes symbolise
both the death of Arcite that will be one result of his contested passion,
and her own eventual loss of virginity and labour as a trophy wife for

Palamon. Even chastity itself is a visceral, painful, fluid-soaked affair in this world, as many of the images in the Temple of Diana suggest. Despite the conventionality of the narrative and its ordered, balanced, representation of events, the poem thus takes an ultimately serious, unsentimentalised view of the role of sexual desire in human affairs, and the painful consequences of its pursuit in a rebarbative universe.

Chaucer mocks the absurdities of Palamon and Arcite's behaviour; but his is a tolerant mockery. Like Theseus, coming across the two fighting furiously in the grove, the narrator is able to combine a sense of detached amusement at the young men's antics ('now looketh, is nat that an heigh folye? / Who may been a fool, but if he love' (1798–9)) with a sense of compassion at the depths of abjection to which love can bring its victims.[44] Although the accidents of their behaviour are mocked, the substance at its core is recognised and endorsed by an authoritative voice who has himself known what it is like to be young and in love ('I woot it myself ful yore agon' (1813)). Again, the contrast with Absolon (whose foolishness lies in the adoption of the accidents of love while remaining entirely ignorant of its substance) is telling.

A second, apparently even closer case will further clarify the crucial differences between the 'romantic' notions of Absolon and those of the true romance hero. In *Sir Gawain and the Green Knight* the attitude to sexuality is also ultimately mature and serious. On one level Gawain's trajectory through the poem mirrors that of Absolon in *The Miller's Tale*. He is a supremely courteous young man, well-versed in the protocols of refined, 'courtly' speech, who encounters a woman seemingly more sexually experienced and uninhibited than himself who outwits him, prompting in him a sudden and violent loathing of the flesh and of his own previously acknowledged sexual identity. But the resemblance is, again, only superficial. While Gawain may be placed in the role of the innocent abroad, and is the butt of some delicate (and some fairly broad) sexual comedy in the bedroom scenes of Fitt Three, and is frequently feminised in his relationship with his active, indeed predatory adversary, he is nonetheless authentic in his emotional responses, a figure of 'earnest' beneath the obvious game-play. It has been suggested that part at least of Gawain's difficulty on the first day of trial may be created by the fact that he is naked beneath the bedcovers and so prevented by modesty from getting up and must endure the symbolic emasculation of being pinned down and trapped

---

[44] Kolve, *Chaucer and the Imagery of Narrative*, pp. 91–3.

by a woman.[45] Yet it is not the embarrassment of being seen naked by a woman *per se* that Gawain fears. His discomfort is social rather than personal, as the repeated references (in a poem playfully willing to acknowledge the knight's pre-existence in other texts) to his sexual experience elsewhere suggest. Rather the awkwardness here is entirely constructed by the obligations inherent upon Gawain's status as a guest, and his need to conform to the protocols of loyalty to his host.

The revulsion that Gawain expresses in the fourth fitt at the promptings of the 'flesh crabbed' are thus directed against his own cowardice and covetousness, the urges that ostensibly prompted him to seek the comfort of the green girdle and the promise of protection that it offered (as he tells Bercilak, 'For care of þy knokke, cowardyse me taȝt / To acorde me with covetyse, my kynde to forsake' (2378–9)) rather than at the stirrings of lust that he felt (see ll. 945ff.) for the woman who is fairer than Guinevere. Similarly the misogynistic outburst against the whole female sex is prompted not by the lady's capacity for sexual betrayal but by her subtlety in tricking him into the ill-advised promise to secrete the girdle. Indeed the former possibility, that Gawain, like Absolon, has resolved hereafter to wash his hands of 'paramours' on account of their treachery, is denied by his wry declaration that the best way with women is 'to luf hom wel and [be]leve hem not' (2421).

Romance, then, retains in both its child-like quality and its capacity for growth, characteristics that distinguish it from Absolon's infantile, essentially inflexible sexual identity. Gawain or Palamon, transposed into *The Miller's Tale*, would not behave in the way that Absolon does. The ability of a romance hero to negotiate the unexpected situations that adventure throws up, his capacity for expressing his sexual desires explicitly, and not least his potential for the kind of devastating physical violence that lies at the heart of chivalric adventuring (the kind of death-dealing that sees Gawain dispose of giants, bandits and wild animals in a single stanza (720–5), and Palamon froth at the mouth like a wild boar while wading ankle-deep in his own blood (*KT*, 1635ff.)): all of these qualities would make him even more mad, bad, and dangerous to know in the unprepared world of bourgeois comedy than he is in his natural romance habitat (where at least everyone is used to sudden death as a regular fact of life). Absolon's own inept attempt to deploy violence in his own cause through the use of the coulter, unchivalrously aimed at a 'defenceless' woman, and even then

---

[45] M. Andrew and R. Waldron, eds, *The Poems of the Pearl Manuscript* (Exeter: Exeter University Press, 1987), pp. 249–79; see also pp. 38–42 for what follows.

mistaking the target, only serves to highlight the contrast. The only 'romance' equivalent to Absolon is Chaucer's other parodic creation, Sir Thopas, another travesty of real romance encoding, who shares the same levels of inadequacy and squeamishness we see in Absolon.[46]

Nor is it the case that Absolon's sexual drives are euphemised or displaced into other symbolic acts or into the imagery that the text deploys around him. Such is the case, for example, in *The Knight's Tale*, where the phallic tower and luxuriant May garden speak eloquently of the protagonists' desires, the extinguished flame and trickle of blood in Diana's temple suggests Emelye's visceral fears concerning the demands of sexual maturity, and the sheer profusion of images of bodily disfigurement in all three temples seems, like Dorian Gray's portrait, to absorb the protagonists' painful knowledge of the likely consequences of being a mortal body in the grip of powerful desire, leaving them to pursue their quests freed of anxiety. Rather Absolon is, as I have suggested, bowdlerised, his squeamishness a sign that his sexuality has been entirely written out of the picture.

Kolve usefully draws attention to the passage in Chaucer's translation of the *Romance of the Rose*, in which the God of Love provides a detailed description of the lot of those who have fallen into his snare. Every true lover, he declares, suffers willingly a solitary confinement of both heart and body in hope of the release that only his beloved can offer. Each is

> . . . as man in prisoun sett,
> And may not geten for to et
> But barly breed, and watir pure,
> And lyeth in vermyn and ordure:
> With all this yitt can he lyve,
> Good hope such comfort hath hym yive,
> Which maketh wene that he shall be
> Delyvered, and come to liberte.
> In fortune is [his] fulle trust;
> Though he lye in strawe or dust,
> In hoope is all his susteynyng.
> And so for lovers, in her wenyng,
> Which Love hath shit in his prisoun.   (2755–67)

---

[46] For an excellent reading of Sir Thopas in these terms, see Jeffrey Jerome Cohen, 'Diminishing Manhood in Chaucer's *Tale of Sir Thopas*', in Beidler, ed., *Masculinities in Chaucer*, pp. 143–55; and C. David Benson, *Chaucer's Drama of Style: Poetic Variety and Contrast in the Canterbury Tales* (Chapel Hill: University of North Carolina Press, 1986), pp. 32–7.

It is precisely the vermin and ordure, the genuine physical suffering, the sheer, corporeal discomfort of being a human being, subject to all the embarrassing functions that flesh is heir to, that Absolon is unwilling to subscribe to – indeed, is incapable of recognising. And it is this that marks out his 'luf-longyng' as inauthentic. Hence it is telling that it is this very corporeality that rears up to refute his pretensions, even as the straw and the dust that are the true lover's metaphorical lot return in material form as the means whereby he seeks to mortify and purify his lips of all trace of Alisoun's likerous 'nether ye'.

Like a Virgin: The Squeamish Body Personified

If Absolon fails in his attempts to play the amatory role that he chooses for himself, however, what about the role that society has chosen for him, that of parish clerk? The general critical consensus has been, unsurprisingly, that he is singularly unsuited for this vocation too. But, in one respect at least, he may not be. His fantasy of Alisoun that is so rudely shattered by the encounter with her nether eye, while sadly out of synch with the reality of fabliau womanhood, does reflect very closely contemporary devotion to another female role model, the Virgin Mary. And, given that one of Absolon's favoured pastimes is playing 'Herodes' on a scaffold high (presumably in pageants of the Magi and the Slaughter of the Innocents) it is intriguing to note that he would have seen played out around him in the Nativity sequence of whatever putative 'Oxford cycle' he took part in, the story of something very like the woman of his dreams.

In surviving dramatic presentations of the Nativity (based upon apocryphal sources such as the *Protoevangelium of St James*, and texts such as the *Revelations* of St Bridget of Sweden), Mary's body and its functions are represented in terms unlikely to offend even the most squeamish of men. The plays present a Virgin who both miraculously defies the normal rules of conception and childbirth and delights the senses in so doing. In the York *Nativity* pageant, for example, the emphasis is on the 'sweetness' and 'comfort' of Christ's birth amid the discomforts of the Bethlehem stable. In its counterpart from the Chester cycle (the second half of Play 6) the birth is described as not merely painless ('withouten teen or travailing' (506)), but acutely pleasurable ('clean maiden this woman is, / for she hath born a child with bliss' (509–10)). And in the York *Purification* pageant St Symeon declares that a degree of that sensual delight extended to all those who either witnessed the event or encountered the Virgin afterwards.

Mary's womb, he confirms, 'yieldyd fresh and fayr / And she a clean vyrgen and unfyld' (356–7), and he praises her, in terms reminiscent of some of Absolon's pastoral flights of fancy, as a virginal meadow flower the odour of whose 'goodness reflars [i.e. rises up] to us all' (366–7).[47]

The N-Town *Nativity* pageant provides the most anatomically detailed version of this phenomenon, when it brings midwives on-stage to testify to the purity and cleanness of Mary's *post-partum* integrity.

> Come nere, gode systyr Salomé.
> Beholde þe brestys of þis clene mayd.
> Ful of fayr mylke how þat þei be;
> And hyre chylde clene, as I fyrst sayd.
> As other ben nowth fowle arayd,
> But clene and pure bothe modyr and chylde   (234–41)

The world in which children are born from pure, sweet-smelling women by painless process of osmosis,[48] without blood, sweat, or amniotic fluids – without, that is, any of the gore, smell, and mess that real physical childbirth entails – and in which young tender virgins dispense wholesome, sweet-tasting milk from their full, rounded breasts as they smile serenely at the viewer, is very much Absolon's fantasy world of amorous lambs at the teat made flesh. As Salome, the first of the N-Town midwives attests, Mary remains, even after child-birth, every inch the perfect woman that she always was, and every bit the sweet-tasting treat that Absolon hoped Alisoun would be,

---

[47] Beadle, ed., *The York Plays*, pp. 125–8 and 151; David Mills, ed., *The Chester Mystery Cycle* (East Lansing: University of Michigan Press, 1992), p. 122.
[48] In Bridget of Sweden's account of the Virgin birth, the process was so perfectly arranged that she professed herself unable to determine even from which orifice the baby emerged. ('And that maner off the byrth was so sothenly and so wysely doone that I myght not dyscerne nor perceyve how or what membyr off her body she had borne her chylde withall', Bridget of Sweden, *The Revelations*, Chapter XII, excerpted in *Women's Writing in Middle English*, ed. by Alexandra Barratt (London: Longman, 1992), p. 87.) Squeamish male theologians had, of course, already hit upon the ideal means of bowdlerising Mary's sexuality in the notion of the *conceptio per aurem*: the idea that Christ was conceived by the Virgin through reception of the Holy Spirit through her ear. Thereby the Marian genitals could be absolved of all sense of through traffic in either direction, and the question of just how, precisely, the Word was made flesh could be tactfully avoided.

a mayde as sche was beforn
Natt fowle polutyd as other women be,
But fayr and fresch as rose on thorn,
Lely-whyte, clene with pure virginyte.   (302–5)

Sadly for Absolon, however, Alisoun proves merely 'fowle polutyd, as other women be'.

That Absolon is not just a jobbing barber and legal scrivener but a parish clerk, is, then, far from incidental to his portrait. Amorous clerks litter the fabliaux, and frequently their failure to achieve their sexual ambitions forms the climax of the comic narrative. Chaucer's neat twist on the tradition is to make his parish clerk not the conventional lecherous hypocrite, using his status as 'gloser' of Holy Writ to seduce his victims, but someone who actually believes what he reads about the ideal woman in the books of the Fathers and what he sees of her in the religious drama. Absolon is not only an inadequate lover whose sexual identity seems to have been constructed from a grotesque misreading of the drama and the spiritual and courtly love lyrics, but a man who expects the woman he pursues to be the same. Having internalised the image of the blessed Virgin as his model of womanhood, he has fashioned his identity in the form best suited to court her. Kara Virginia Donaldson usefully observes that 'Alisoun is both the product and object of a male discourse that has maintained power over women by separating women from both their bodies and language.' But it is important to note that, in Absolon, Chaucer offers a male character created in the same way. As Donaldson further suggests, one of the most effective rhetorical strategies of medieval courtly love poetry lies in the way it addresses the female object of desire as though she were the Virgin. The only difference here is that with Absolon there is no pretence, no cynical seductive agenda behind the surface courtesies.[49]

In this respect, Absolon's portrayal fits the wider agenda of the narrative he inhabits. *The Miller's Tale* itself, as a number of critics have pointed out, plays irreverently with the Virgin's *vita*, offering in the triangle of Alisoun, John the carpenter, and Nicholas a comic variant of the trio of Mary, Joseph, and the Angel Gabriel at the Annunciation.[50] The echoes are, of course, pointed up by the fact that it is the *Angelus ad virginem* that Nicholas sings lustily in his room at nights. In

---

[49] Donaldson, 'Alisoun's Language', pp. 141 and 145.
[50] Beryl Rowland, 'Chaucer's Blasphemous Churl: A New Interpretation of the *Miller's Tale*', in *Chaucer and Middle English Studies in Honour of Rossell Hope Robbins*, ed. by B. Rowland (London: Allen & Unwin, 1974), pp. 43–55.

treating the Virgin's story comically in this way, Chaucer was, it seems, following the lead of the dramatists (although the precise chronology of composition is not clear), who had in the pageant of *Joseph's Trouble about Mary* already imagined a grotesque realist reading of the Annunciation in Joseph's suspicion that 'som man in aungellis liknesse / With somkyn gawde has hir begiled' (*Joseph's Troubles*, York, 136–7), leaving her pregnant and her impotent husband facing humiliation. Rather than dissolve such doubts with the arrival of a manifestly authentic angel as the pageant-makers did, however, Chaucer allows the counter-narrative to play itself out, with Nicholas in the role of the beguiling young man. What *The Miller's Tale* adds to the scenario is the figure of Absolon, who provides the fulcrum around which the Annunciation story is swung into parody. While Joseph is transformed into an avaricious cuckold, Gabriel into a lecherous student, and Mary herself into a wild and 'likerous' young wife, the parish clerk remains the repository of the values of the 'orthodox' story, maladroitly retaining its sense of the numinous potential within the mundane, begging for a kiss 'For Jhesus love, and for the love of me' (3717), and voicing his courtship in terminology borrowed from the Song of Songs and contemporary lyrics. While both Nicholas and Alisoun have adopted the carapace of cynicism necessary for survival in the fabliau world, only Absolon (and to a degree John, the other dupe of the story) continues to see the world with a child's eyes, as do the characters in the Nativity sequence of the cycle plays.

What *The Miller's Tale* seems to be mocking is thus not the use of inappropriate language to couch sexual ambition, as is assumed by those readings that place Absolon's humiliation in the context of the Miller's 'quiting' of *The Knight's Tale*, but the inappropriate erasing of sexuality – and corporeality *per se* – that is an explicit part of the religious drama and of Mariolatry generally. In this respect Absolon is the fabliau world's response to the suggestion that the only possible reaction to the Mother of God was a reversion to childhood, and a denial of sexuality (if God Himself could become a child for this woman, the argument seems to run, how much more compelling is the need for her mortal admirers to infantilise themselves before her?). The issue clearly interested Chaucer, as his other problematic excursion into Mariolatry, *The Prioress's Prologue* and *Tale*, involves a similar process of infantilisation, this time of both the protagonist, the little 'clergeon', and the narrator herself, reduced to the status of 'a child of twelf month oold, or lesse' (484) in the face of the Virgin's majestic 'worthynesse'.

What lay behind this interest in the powerful nexus of ideas of adoration, infantilisation, squeamishness and denied sexuality is, of course, another question entirely. That Chaucer should fashion so contemptible a vehicle as Absolon for such notions raises more problems than it solves. One could, of course, attribute that contempt to Chaucer himself. It would not be unreasonable to posit a poet who reacted violently against the kind of mawkish sentimentality that often characterised popular Mariolatry and frequently tumbled over into a kind of pious pornography obsessed with the details of the Virgin's intact hymen, her fragrant womb, or the sweet perfection of her breasts.[51] Alternatively, one could, following Beryl Rowland, see this as just another aspect of Chaucerian ventriloquism, the crafting of a suitably churlish persona to characterise the Miller, the teller of the first of his churlish tales.[52] Or is it, perhaps, best to see the portrayal of Absolon as one more product of the poet's interest in genres? One might profitably site the contempt for Mariolatry and the squeamish, infantilised males who practise it, squarely within the fabliau spirit itself. For fabliau is a genre in which all relations can be ultimately traced back to sexuality and sexual desire, and from its perspective such attitudes as the Nativity plays express were an explicit denial of reality that needed ridiculing out of court. Either way, Absolon, far from being an afterthought, a comic digression in the narrative of *The Miller's Tale*, represents a fundamental element in both the tale and Chaucer's conception of the fabliau world, and asking why we laugh at him in the way(s) that we do, presents a provocative challenge to our understanding of both gender and genre in medieval culture.

In a sense, then, asking questions about Absolon's own gender position or sexuality is to miss the point. He is not constructed in the way that he is in order to mock a particular kind of man, whether gay or straight, sexually inexperienced or lecherous, but as a repository for certain ideas about women and sexuality drawn from a particular

---

[51] See, for example, a number of the lyrics examined in Douglas Gray, *Themes and Images in the Medieval English Religious Lyric* (London: Routledge, 1972), especially pp. 84–106. Quite how securely *The Prioress's Prologue* and *Tale* fit with this idea is, however, difficult to gauge. The *Tale*, with its attendant prayer to the Virgin, seems on one level to be an authentic exercise in Marian devotion, yet it deploys a similarly eroticised vocabulary to describe how the Virgin, at the Conception, 'ravyshedst doun from the Deitee . . . / . . . the goost that in th[ee] alight' (1659–60). I am very grateful to David Salter for sharing with me his astute comments about *The Prioress's Tale* in this context.
[52] Rowland, 'Chaucer's Blasphemous Churl', p. 44.

genre of literature. If the text deploys homophobic or misogynist motifs, if it seems to laugh laddishly at small instruments and squeamish aversions to farting (and I would argue that it clearly does all of these things) it does not do so in order to mock effeminacy, sexual naïvety, or squeamishness *per se*. Rather it constructs Absolon from a mass of assumptions about sexuality and gender, masculinity and bodily functions, gleaned from popular religious culture, in a way that invites reflection on the demands of that genre itself. Just as the varieties of masculinity displayed by Nicholas and John the Carpenter, Palamon and Arcite, and the other heroes and protagonists discussed in this essay are the product of the needs of fabliau and romance respectively, so Absolon is constructed to display the kind of masculinity called forth by Mariolatry and popular dramatic representations of the Annunciation and the Nativity. He is placed in the jarringly inappropriate genre of the fabliau in order to show up his idiosyncrasies all the more clearly. In doing so Chaucer deploys the fabliau form for a purpose well beyond the normal range of its resonances and implications. If, *The Miller's Tale* seems to argue, one accepts that all women can, and indeed should be like the Virgin, then one must also accept that all men could, indeed should be like Absolon: a prospect the tale treats as so absurd as to demand our laughter.

The Stereotype Confirmed?
Chaucer's Wife of Bath

ELAINE TREHARNE

'I write woman: woman must write woman. And man, man'[1]

Introduction: Methods of Analysis

THIS ESSAY WILL FOCUS on one of the most memorable English literary
characters: Chaucer's Wife of Bath. I shall be taking a primarily
sociolinguistic approach in interpreting her: drawing out interactions
between language and gender, language and power that are as relevant
now as they always have been in male-female relations, and in
engendering and maintaining the powerful ideologies that drive both
the social construction of identity and academic discourses of character
and morality.

The complexity of interpreting Chaucer's *Canterbury Tales* arguably
forms a major impetus for continuing to study the poet and his most
famous work. As well as bringing to life his cast of pilgrims on their
journey to Canterbury, Chaucer provides us with a multiplicity of
generically and stylistically varied tales to entertain and engage us. The
polyphony of the author, narrator, tale-tellers, and characters within
the tales leads to a layered narrative in which the least distinguishable
voice is that of the author. When readers seek to determine what the
meanings of the text might be, both within its contemporary context,
and to the modern reader, this obscurity of the author inevitably
problematises any act of interpretation.

So it is that there is little that can be definitive in reading and
interpreting Chaucer. This, naturally, is ideal fodder for critics, and
among Chaucer's many controversial characters, one of the most
ultimately indefinable is the Wife of Bath.

---

[1] Hélène Cixous, 'The Laugh of the Medusa: New French Feminisms' (1976),
trans. Keith Cohen and Paula Cohen, cited in *Feminist Literary Theory: A
Reader*, ed. by Mary Eagleton, 2nd ed. (Oxford: Blackwell, 1996), p. 322.

Critical Response to the Wife of Bath

Critical response to the Wife of Bath has been as diverse as it has been emotive. Early commentators such as William Blake found her to be 'a scourge and a blight'. He went on to comment that he 'shall say no more of her, nor expose what Chaucer has left hidden; let the young reader study what he has said of her: it is useful as a scare-crow. There are of such characters born too many for the peace of the world.'[2] Of the Wife's *Prologue* itself, Dryden comments that: 'I translated *Chaucer* first [before Boccaccio], and among the rest pitch'd on the Wife of *Bath*'s Tale; not daring, as I have said, to adventure on her Prologue; because 'tis too licentious.'[3]

From these early, slightly prudish comments, twentieth-century criticism emerged to illustrate a continuing controversy in scholarly response, particularly to the Wife of Bath as a character. Kittredge's famous article on 'Chaucer's Discussion of Marriage' reveals (under the guise of the Clerk's anticipated response) that 'The woman was an heresiarch, or at best a schismatic. She set up, and aimed to establish, a new and dangerous sect, whose principle was that the wife should rule the husband . . . She had garnished her sermon with scraps of Holy Writ and rags and tatters of erudition, caught up, we may infer, from her last husband.'[4]

More recently, Tony Slade reaches a similarly critical judgement, claiming that 'The Wife's character has already been exposed in some detail in her Prologue, which rambles around the theme of "sover-eynetee" in marriage; her tone is coarse and garrulous, and there is little evidence of that sort of delicate poetic beauty which some critics have professed to find in the Tale itself.'[5]

Notably, these unfavourable readings are by male critics. One of the most significant developments in the interpretation of the Wife of Bath has come from those women (and some male) critics seeking to

[2] William Blake, A *Descriptive Catalogue of Pictures, Poetical and Historical Inventions, Painted by William Blake* (1809), cited in 'Early Appreciations', in *Chaucer: The Canterbury Tales*, ed. by J. J. Anderson, Casebook Series (London: Macmillan, 1974), p. 39.
[3] John Dryden, Preface to *Fables Ancient and Modern* (1700), in 'Early Appreciations', in *Chaucer: The Canterbury Tales*, p. 31.
[4] G. L. Kittredge, 'Chaucer's Discussion of Marriage', repr. in *Chaucer: The Canterbury Tales*, pp. 61–92, at p. 66.
[5] Tony Slade, 'Irony in the *Wife of Bath*'s Tale', repr. in *Chaucer: The Canterbury Tales*, pp. 160–71, at p. 162.

appropriate the Wife for feminist scholarship in the last three decades. These responses have extended across the full range of critical approaches, incorporating the psychoanalytic, the New Historicist or Cultural Materialist, to deconstructive affective stylistic and reader-response theory.[6] Such methodologies have yielded readings of the Wife that see her as a shrewd businesswoman[7] in an emergent bourgeoisie, a 'master of parody'[8] providing a corrective to the 'truths' of conventional authorities; or a 'proto-feminist',[9] an early independently minded woman seeking to reject oppressive patriarchy.

In discussing the manner in which the Wife engages with the writings of the anti-feminists cited throughout her *Prologue*, and takes issue with the ways in which women in contemporary medieval society are portrayed, Jill Mann comments that:

> The double structure of the Wife's speech thus has a meaning of far wider import than its role in the Wife's individual experience. And yet it plays a crucial role in creating our sense of the Wife as a living individual. For what it demonstrates is her *interaction* with the stereotypes of her sex, and it is in this interaction that we feel the three-dimensionality of her existence. That is, she does not live in the insulated laboratory world of literature, where she is no more than a literary object, unconscious of the interpretations foisted upon her; she is conceived as a woman who lives in the real world, in full awareness of the anti-feminist literature that purports to describe and criticise her behaviour, and she has an attitude to *it* just as it has an attitude to her.[10]

Further, citing Patterson's phrase, Mann comments that 'Chaucer could not invent a new "female language", and sensibly did not try to do so . . . but . . . the Wife's Prologue is designed precisely to make

---

[6] Many of these perspectives are well exemplified in Ruth Evans and Lesley Johnson, ed., *Feminist Readings in Middle English Literature: The Wife of Bath and All Her Sect* (London: Routledge, 1994). The editors' Introduction (pp. 1–21), in particular, situates recent scholarship within the overall context of feminist criticism.

[7] Mary Carruthers, 'The Wife of Bath and the Painting of Lions', repr. with a new 'Afterword' in *Feminist Readings*, pp. 22–53.

[8] Carruthers, 'The Wife of Bath', p. 26.

[9] See, for example, Marion Wynne-Davies, '"The Elf-Queen with Hir Joly Compaignye": Chaucer's *Wife of Bath's Tale*', in *Women and Arthurian Literature: Seizing the Sword*, ed. by Marion Wynne-Davies (New York: St Martin's Press, 1996), pp. 14–35.

[10] Jill Mann, *Geoffrey Chaucer* (London: Harvester Wheatsheaf, 1991), p. 79.

the reader conscious of the confining nature of "the prison house of masculine language".'[11]

While there is a good deal of truth in these statements, I would suggest that Chaucer does nonetheless attempt to 'invent a new female language' inasmuch as he provides a voice for the Wife that deliberately attempts to emulate aspects of a woman's language, albeit from an entirely stereotypically conceived basis. Moreover, the textual dissemination of the authorities against which she speaks was such that the access she has had to them can only have come through an interpretative mediator – her fifth husband Jankyn with his impromptu evenings spent vernacularising the Latin *auctoritas* contained within the antifeminist writings. Not only, then, does the Wife internalise the interpreted words of the Church Fathers, but she re-interprets them, uttering them in a language – English – that was itself marginalised, Other: in so doing, she further marginalises herself even as she seeks to situate herself within the realm of the authoritative.

Problematising the issue of verbal and social intercourse, the Wife is interpreted by Barrie Ruth Straus from a psychoanalytic perspective as 'participating in a homosexual exchange with the Pardoner' in the course of her *Prologue*, following the Pardoner's interruption. 'Under the guise of sharing with men the secret of the feigned appetite as one of women's ways of handling men, the Wife articulates the homoerotic nature of phallocentric sexuality: that it is masculine desire seeking only itself. When she makes the Pardoner her accomplice in betraying her husbands' secrets, she in effect puts the Pardoner in bed with her and her husbands.'[12]

While this reading is puzzling, Straus's overall evaluation of the Wife is one that foregrounds the opacity of the text: that 'The Wife of Bath is the uncontrollable voice that eludes interpretative truth. The ultimate secret she reveals is that all who think they can control, penetrate, and master such texts as she represents are deluded. All the critics can do is create interpretations that double their own desire.'[13] It surely is the case that the crucial aspect of Chaucer's work is the demands made on the readers' own interpretation and moral response. As Chauncey Wood succinctly puts it: 'it is not the text that produces

---

[11] Mann, *Chaucer*, p. 80.
[12] Barrie Ruth Straus, 'Subversive Discourse of the Wife of Bath: Phallocentric Discourse and the Imprisonment of Criticism', repr. in *Chaucer: Contemporary Critical Essays*, ed. by Valerie Allen and Aers Axiotis, New Casebooks (London: Macmillan, 1997), pp. 126–44 (at p. 133).
[13] Straus, 'Subversive Discourse of the Wife of Bath', p. 142.

readings but the readings that produce the text.'[14] But here, certainly in Straus's argument, and elsewhere in other scholarly comments, the critic appears to perceive the Wife as the shaper of her own *Prologue* and *Tale*, as a 'voice' that effectively propagandises a new 'truth'. Lynne Dickson, for example, argues that:

> Despite textual signals that Alison tries to control and disempower the antifeminist topos, it ultimately overwhelms her. The sheer length of her *Prologue* and the fact that she loses her train of thought six times support the reading that Alison experiences considerable discomfort with her speaking situation. One of the *Prologue*'s strategies, then, seems to be to expose the tyranny of masculine discourse: it oppresses even a figure like Alison. This revelation is complemented by the text's method of hailing its reader as more complicated and open than the oppressively monolithic audience that Alison cannot escape.[15]

And it is this that strikes me as most problematic: to read the Wife as if she were anything other than a fiction masterfully created by Chaucer is to fall into the trap of 'truth' that he sets through his vivid, realistic depictions.

There is no doubt that Chaucer ventriloquises his female fiction effectively. The Wife's is a voice that resonates loudly in Middle English literature, and that assists in making her stand out as one of the most memorable of all female literary characters. It is precisely this multi-layered speech-act that permits for a sociolinguistic analysis employing theories of language and power, and language and gender to determine the possible nature of the characterisation of the Wife, and the potential acuity of and purpose in Chaucer's depiction.

---

[14] Chauncey Wood, 'Affective Stylistics and the Study of Chaucer', *Studies in the Age of Chaucer* 6 (1984), 21–40 (at p. 39).

[15] Lynne Dickson, 'Deflection in the Mirror: Feminine Discourse in *The Wife of Bath's Prologue and Tale*', *Studies in the Age of Chaucer* 15 (1993), p. 79. Dickson does go on to say that 'Drawing lines between the fictional and the actual in *The Wife's Prologue* is problematic because Alison herself is not an actual speaking woman but a fictional construct' (p.85, n.50). There should not, of course, be any difficulty 'drawing lines between the fictional and the actual' since the entire *Prologue* is a fiction however realistically the fiction might be portrayed.

Folklinguistic Stereotypes of Women's Language

Sociolinguistics is the modern study of the ways in which language operates within society. It emerged, in part, from Saussure's analyses of language in the earlier part of the twentieth century, and the movement away from more historical modes of language analysis such as philology, dominant in the nineteenth century. Through sociolinguistic experiment, it has proven possible to determine, for example, the use by particular groups of speakers of variant forms of language. Where this usage correlates to a social, economical, or gendered group, relationships between language and power, language and class, and language and gender can be determined and analysed. The discipline, in principle, is not a judgemental one: no values are notionally placed on the results; rather, it collects and collates empirical data about variability within language and possible determining features.[16]

There is no question about Chaucer's own language awareness. In *The Reeve's Tale*, the two students, John and Aleyn, are of Northern origin. Their speech is peppered with Northernisms that are interpreted by the editors of *The Riverside Chaucer* as 'apparently the first case of this kind of joking imitation of a dialect recorded in English literature'.[17] Chaucer thus attempts, with relative success, the phonetic representation of variant forms of English within his text. Taking a wider linguistic perspective, Chaucer demonstrates himself to be very conscious of his role as a transmitter of the vernacular, at a time when its prestige as a vehicle for literary production had yet to be firmly established. In his lengthy Romance, *Troilus and Criseyde*, Chaucer's narrator comments:

[16] See, for example, Ronald Wardhaugh, *An Introduction to Sociolinguistics*, 2nd ed. (Oxford: Blackwell, 1992).

[17] *The Reeve's Tale*, lines 4084–9, for example, illustrate a multitude of Northern spellings, emboldened in the quotation below:

> "Allas," quod John, "Aleyn, for Cristes peyne
> Lay doun thy swerd, and I wil myn **alswa**.
> I is ful **wight**, God **waat**, as is a **raa**;
> By Goddes herte, he **sal** nat scape us **bathe**!
> Why ne had thow **pit** the capul in the **lathe**?
> Ilhayl! By God, Alayn, thou is a fonne!"

All quotations are taken from Larry D. Benson, ed., *Riverside Chaucer*, 3rd ed. (Oxford: Oxford University Press, 1987), unless otherwise stated. The quotation commenting on dialect in *The Reeve's Tale* is from the *Riverside Chaucer*, p. 850b.

And for ther is so gret diversite
In Englissh and in writyng of oure tonge,
So prey I God that non myswrite the,
Ne the mysmetre for defaute of tonge;
And red wherso thow be, or elles songe,
That thow be understonde, God I biseche![18]

Furthermore, Chaucer's awareness of literary form is not only evident from his manipulation of it within *The Canterbury Tales*' variety and versatility, but also from his comments through the voice of the Parson of the associations of alliterative verse in contemporary England:

But trusteth wel, I am a Southren man;
I kan nat geeste 'rum, ram, ruf', by letter,
Ne, God woot, rym holde I but litel better;
And therefore, if yow list – I wol nat glose –
I wol yow telle a myrie tale in prose[19]

Chaucer's mockery of this poetic form in the mouth of the prose-telling, truth-telling Parson illustrates clearly the author's own linguistic acuity and observation.

The demands of ostensibly telling the truth by repeating the (fictional) words of the characters in his writing result in Chaucer's creation of a variety of realistic voices, each of which is suited in varying degrees to a particular pilgrim narrator. In the case of the majority of the pilgrims, the men, Chaucer's main concern may have been the representation of a register appropriate to each narrator; for example, in the choice of doctrinaire prose for the Parson; the courtly language and rhyme royal versification of the Knight in his philosophical romance; the classically-infused religious register of the Monk throughout his episodic tragedy; and the bawdy language and frequent colloquialisms uttered by the Miller in his complex fabliau. In the case of the three women who tell tales, however, the Wife of Bath, the Prioress, and the Second Nun, Chaucer has not only to find a register and style suitable to their respective status, but also an appropriate means of imitating the language usage of women.

It has long been the case that the perceived differences between men's use of language and women's have been thought worthy of judgemental comment, especially by male scholars and writers. These

---

[18] *Troilus and Criseyde*, lines 1792–9.
[19] *The Parson's Tale*, lines 42–6.

differences have until very recently been noted in order to indicate women's irritating habits, their deviancy or inadequacy in language usage in comparison to the norm – that is, men's language usage.[20] This 'inferior' use by women of language is, of course, part of the paradigm of the social and familial subjugation of women, for perceived inequality in language usage reflects and contributes to actual inequality in society. Such attitudes to women's speech – that women are not as adept at language usage, or that there are particular forms of language use more appropriate to women – persist, however, in phrases such as 'girls' talk', or 'women talk too much', or 'ladies shouldn't swear'.

The myths surrounding women's use of language are ancient in origin, and their constancy and ubiquity is testimony to the stability of a social order which has undoubtedly been, until relatively recently, patriarchal, institutionally controlled, and exclusive. Chaucer's linguistic awareness yields interesting results in terms of his use of then-current (and in many cases still current), folklinguistic or anecdotal accounts of women as speakers. His ventriloquism as the Wife of Bath, and indeed as the Prioress and Second Nun, offers ideal material for analysis using socio-linguistic theory, and leads to the conclusion that he was very much immersed in, and quite content to perpetuate, the stereotypes of women's language use prevalent in late medieval academic (and therefore male) culture. An evaluation of the female pilgrims becomes, consequently, not so much a matter of what they say, but of how they say it.

Although Chaucer himself has been regarded by some scholars as a proto-feminist writer, this seems akin to anachronistic wishful think-ing. Better, it seems, if one wants to regard him as proto-anything, is the conception of Chaucer as a proto-sociolinguist, or more properly perhaps, proto-folklinguist. He is a writer whose fictional creations deliberately raise issues of the relationship between language and social structures, and who question implicitly the status quo in crucial cultural relationships such as language and gender.

Before I outline the major aspects of mythical language use by women

---

[20] The derogatory comments of male commentators on women's language subsequently led to the proposition that women's language is powerless, indicative of women's inferiority in verbal communication. In recent years, this 'powerlessness' has been reappraised and shown to be demonstrative of women's communicative strengths of co-operation, lucidity, and solidarity. See, for example, Dale Spender, *Man Made Language* (London: Routledge, 1980), Deborah Cameron, *Feminism and Linguistic Theory* (London: Macmillan, 1985), and Jennifer Coates, *Women, Men and Language*, 2nd ed. (London: Macmillan, 1993).

incorporated by Chaucer into his depiction of the Wife of Bath, I should like to offer a word of caution to allay any suspicions that my focus on this methodology may have prompted. First, sociolinguistic analysis focuses mostly on *parole*, that is the actual *spoken* utterance, and here, I will be applying it to written language, and moreover, a fairly formal versified language. Even so, it is a relevant approach, since Chaucer the author through his pilgrim narrator is claiming to be repeating the actual spoken words of his subject, the Wife of Bath. Second, sociolinguistics often analyses language synchronically. However, as it assists in explaining relations between language users and society, it can most fruitfully be used diachronically in order to illustrate and elucidate power relations in society at any given point in social evolution.

Perhaps the primary linguistic determinants of women's language, and it should be noted that these are also folklinguistic,[21] are that women gossip, nag, verbally harass, give bad advice, cannot be trusted, and talk uncontrollably. This myth could be evinced by very considerable numbers of quotations from texts, both ancient and modern. The twelfth-century *Proverbs of Alfred*, numbers fifteen and sixteen,[22] for example, reveal that:

> þus queþ Alvred:
> 'Ne wurþ þu never so wod
> Ne so wyn-drunke,
> þat evere segge þine wife
> Alle þine wille.
> For if þu iseye þe bivore
> þine ivo alle,
> And þu hi myd worde
> Iwreþþed hevedest,
> Ne scholde heo hit lete
> For þing lyvyinde,
> þat heo ne scholde þe forþ upbreyde
> Of þine baleusyþes.
> Wymmon is word-wod,
> And haveþ tunge to swift;
> þeyh heo wel wolde,
> Ne may heo hi nowiht welde.'

[21] That is, long perpetuated myths, which are still highly visible in social interaction and communication today, and to which this author does not, in any way, subscribe.
[22] Elaine Treharne, ed., *Old and Middle English: An Anthology* (Oxford: Blackwell, 2000), pp. 364–5.

> . . . þe mon þat let wymmon
> His mayster iwurþe,
> Ne schal he never beon ihurd
> His wordes loverd;
> Ac heo hine schal steorne
> Totrayen and toteone,
> And selde wurþ he blyþe and gled
> þe mon þat is his wives qued.
> Mony appel is bryht wiþute
> And bitter wiþinne;
> So is mony wymmon
> On hyre fader bure
> Schene under schete,
> And þeyh heo is schendful.

In these proverbs, erroneously ascribed to King Alfred, and surviving in a number of thirteenth-century manuscripts, oft-repeated criticisms of women's language usage are iterated. Women are 'word-wod' ('word-mad' or 'wild in speech') and cannot be trusted to hold their tongue; an infuriated wife's prolixity will inevitably result in her public reprimanding of the unfortunate husband in front of even his worst enemies; and women in general simply cannot control their verbosity, even if they try to. Such commonplace and stereotypical myths about women's language usage are entirely bound up, from the male perspective, with a woman's trustworthiness, her discretion, and her overall demeanour and appearance.

Such proverbial derogations of women's language, and the inevitable allying of 'shrewishness' with a more general female proclivity to unfortunate and unacceptable habits, are explicit in Chaucer. The Merchant, for example, tells his (clearly male) audience to: 'Suffre thy wyves tonge, as Catoun bit; / She shal comande, and thou shal suffren it';[23] and the host adds to *The Merchant's Tale*, that:

> I have a wyf, though she povre be,
> But of hir tonge a labbyng shrewe is she,
> And yet she hath an heep of vices mo;[24]

Women's loquaciousness thus becomes symptomatic of their general urge to 'comande' with the consequence that the male recipient –

---

[23] *The Merchant's Tale*, lines 1377–8.
[24] The Epilogue to *The Merchant's Tale*, lines 2427–9.

usually the husband – must endure excessive torment as a result. This insidious stereotyping of women,[25] and wives in particular, is endemic in the writings of medieval male authors. Elements of this folklinguistic myth to which women have been subject are ancient, and develop in part from the most authoritative of sources, the Bible. In I Timothy 2.11–14, for instance, St Paul asserts: 'Let the woman learn in silence, with all subjection. But I suffer not a woman to teach, nor to usurp authority over the man; but to be in silence. For Adam was first formed; then Eve. And Adam was not seduced, but the woman, being seduced, was in the transgressions.' From such scripture and subsequent exegesis, therefore, emerges the ideal woman: a silent one.[26] 'It is possible to go even further and to suggest that when women are supposed to be quiet, a talkative woman is one who talks at all.'[27]

This is the easiest myth to evidence as replicated by Chaucer in his creation. The Wife has by far the longest *Prologue* in the *Tales*, and one where the narratorial subjectivity is more pronounced than elsewhere, other than the feminised Pardoner's *Prologue*. Moreover, confirming the stereotype of the verbose woman are the speeches within the speech by which the Wife recalls her own words to her husbands, condemning the successive husbands' anti-feminist commonplaces, while simultaneously confirming them. The myths of women's inability to maintain privacy, their tendency to gossip, and to speak of 'trivial' matters – such as love and relationships – are shown to be part of the operative mode of the Wife. When she discusses Jankyn, who went to board with her friend Alison, we learn that the Wife tells Alison everything:

> She knew myn herte, and eek my privetee,
> Bet that oure parrisshe preest, so moot I thee!
> To hire biwreyed I my conseil al.
> For hadde myn housbonde pissed on a wal,
> Or doon a thing that sholde han cost his lyf,
> To hire, and to another worthy wyf,
> And to my nece, which that I loved weel,
> I wolde han toold his conseil every deel.

[25] In Passus V of *Piers Plowman*, for example, the sin of Wrath tells his audience that he has encouraged the malicious gossip and 'wicked words' of nuns while employed as their cook. See A. V. C. Schmidt, ed., *William Langland: A Critical Edition of the B-Text* (London: Dent Everyman, 1978), Passus V, lines 151–63.
[26] As discussed by Jennifer Coates, *Women, Men and Language*, pp. 33–6, illustrated by a number of medieval and Renaissance literary sources.
[27] Spender, *Man Made Language*, p. 43.

> And so I did ful often, God it woot,
> That made his face often reed and hoot
> For verray shame, and blamed himself for he
> Had tool to me so greet a pryvetee.[28]

Here, the Wife takes obvious pride in recounting her indiscretions
that occur 'ful often', not only to her best friend, but also to another
woman, and to her niece. These intimate news reports include the
revelation of secrets told to her by her husband, even those where
disclosure would have cost him dearly. Her delight in these activities,
no matter how positively they can be read,[29] serves to confirm the
stereotype of the 'gossiping' woman, incapable of remaining discreet,
incapable of earning trust. The Wife's pleasure and self-approval in
these activities, the lack of censure she appears to receive, reinforces
those proverbs and myths that warn men of the danger of telling
women their secrets, and then subsequently blame the same men for
the foolishness they show in trusting their wives. Such confirmation
of the 'truths' about women (and, one might add here, too-trusting
men) perpetuated by male authors like Chaucer actually weakens the
Wife's position, and stereotypes her even as she tries to throw the
anti-feminist stereotyping back at her husbands. And, while the
length of the *Prologue* itself is the most obvious evidence of the
woman's mythical inability to be brief, Chaucer invites us to look
more closely at the Wife's language through the ample amount of
evidence he provides for her in mimicking the voice of the late
fourteenth-century widow. Her *Prologue*, in effect, becomes a handbook to observations on women's language, some five hundred years
before a sustained thesis was advanced.

---

[28] *The Wife of Bath's Prologue*, lines 531–42.
[29] Some critics have read this narration of the Wife's network of female friends
as demonstrating the close and powerful communities that women formed in
this period. This may well, indirectly, be the case, but it remains that Chaucer
is depicting here a less-than-positive picture of women's volubility as the norm.
Susan Signe Morrison, 'Don't Ask, Don't Tell: The Wife of Bath and
Vernacular Translations', *Exemplaria* 8 (1996), 97–123, discusses this same
passage at pp. 115–16, and suggests at p. 116 that: 'The anxiety the Wife's
husband feels reflects the anxiety felt among those men who opposed
vernacular translations; once privileged men no longer maintained exclusive
access to knowledge, society itself would be threatened with subversion'; and at
p. 117, 'the ability or tendency for women to reveal secrets only heightens their
own power'.

Language and Gender

When Otto Jespersen wrote his famous book on language and its
origins in 1922,[30] he ostensibly presented empirical evidence to
validate his work. In his chapter entitled 'Woman' (with, significantly,
as pointed out by various later twentieth-century linguists, no compar-
able chapter for 'Man'),[31] he signalled that women's language requires
its own discussion and set of comments, because it is not the norm;
rather, it is to be measured against the normative language usage of the
white, middle-class male. Chaucer's lengthy characterisation of the
Wife of Bath similarly marks her out as beyond the norm. While this
positively questions social roles, it also highlights the manner in which
the Wife is outside; in providing the Wife with an opportunity to talk
about herself at a length and in a manner not afforded to any other
pilgrim, Chaucer marks her out as 'unusual' or 'remarkable' (in a
positive reading) and as 'deviant' (in a negative). As she is representative of the non-standard, it is almost inevitable that she can be read as
being depicted derogatorily in comparison with the norm,[32] particularly
within the fourteenth-century cultural and social contexts of male
dominance and female subordination.

Jespersen and Chaucer have a good deal in common as proponents of
folklinguistic stereotyping of women's language: Jespersen provides a
list of the folklinguistic myths to which sociolinguists in the 1970s and
1980s felt compelled to reply, and not always with a rebuttal. Much of
Jespersen's 'evidence' is based on anecdote rather than objective and
empirical observation, but it is cited as (his) truth because of the
permeation of long-held derogatory views about women's language
usage. Similarly, Chaucer is able to manipulate stereotypical facets of
women's language usage through his creation, and he, to a significant

[30] Otto Jespersen, *Language, Its Nature, Development, and Origin* (London:
Allen and Unwin, 1922). Chapter XIII is devoted to 'The Woman'.
[31] See, for example, Coates, *Women, Men and Language*, pp. 18–20; Dale
Spender, *Man Made Language*, pp. 10–11.
[32] As Jenkins and Kramarae state: 'Both the theory and the methodology [of
the stratification approach taken by sociolinguists] are based on the implicit
assumption that the communicative experience of white middle class males is
prototypical . . . the experience of women, other ethnic groups and classes are
treated as deviations', cited in *Feminist Linguistic Theory*, ed. by Deborah
Cameron (London: Macmillan, 1985), p. 45, from Mercilee Jenkins and
Cheris Kramarae, 'A Thief in the House: The Case of Women and Language',
in *Men's Studies Modified*, ed. Dale Spender (London: Pergamon, 1981), p. 16.

extent, pre-empts in a literary framework what Jespersen would go on to write within a linguistic structure some five hundred and more years later.

Jespersen's account of women's language provides a blueprint for the promulgation of folklinguistic stereotyping, iterating commonplaces about women's particular characteristics of language usage that owe more to the medieval proverb than they do to the objective collation of data. Among the key features he notes are the divergences between the 'lower and higher registers of language':

> The difference between the two 'languages' is one of degree only: they are two strata of the same language, one higher, more solemn, stiff and archaic, and another lower, more natural and familiar, and this easy, or perhaps we should say slipshod, style is the only one recognized for ordinary women.[33]

He goes on to discuss the use of hyperbolic lexis and intonation in women's speech:

> Another tendency noticed in the language of . . . women is pretty widely spread among French and English women, namely, the excessive use of intensive words and the exaggeration of stress and tone-accent to mark emphasis.[34]

This he expands upon with the remarkable series of examples and explanations:

> the fondness of women for hyperbole will very often lead the fashion with regard to adverbs of intensity, and these are very often used with disregard of their proper meaning . . . There is another intensive which has something of the eternally feminine about it, namely *so* . . . The explanation of this characteristic feminine usage is, I think, that women much more often than men break off without finishing their sentences, because they start talking without having thought out what they are going to say.[35]

This hyperbole of intensifiers helps assist, perhaps, in making more emphatic and startling the woman's subject of discourse, because,

---

[33] Jespersen, *Language, Its Nature, Development, and Origin*, p. 242.
[34] Ibid., p. 243.
[35] Ibid., p. 250.

according to Jespersen, women are incapable of what might be loosely termed 'straight-talking'; hence, their preference for euphemism:

> But when . . . we come to . . . vocabulary and style, we shall find a much greater number of differences . . . There is certainly no doubt, however, that women in all countries are shy of mentioning certain parts of the human body and certain natural functions by the direct and often rude denominations which men, and especially young men, prefer when among themselves. Women will therefore invent innocent and euphemistic words and paraphrases, which sometimes may in the long run come to be looked upon as the plain or blunt names, and therefore in their turn have to be avoided and replaced by more decent words.[36]

Considering that women are so innovative in language, having to 'invent innocent . . . words and phrases', it comes as something of a surprise to discover that:

> the vocabulary of a woman as a rule is much less extensive than that of a man . . . Woman as a rule follows the main road of language, where man is often inclined to turn aside into a narrow footpath or even to strike out a new path for himself . . . Those who want to learn a foreign language will therefore always do well at the first stage to read many ladies' novels, because there they will continually meet with just those everyday words and combinations which the foreigner is above all in need of, what may be termed the indispensable small-change of a language.[37]

The fact that women are adept at the 'small change' of language, that they talk before they have thought through what they are going to say, and that they pepper their speech with intensifiers and phatic words, is summarised by Jespersen's general explanation:

> The volubility of women has been the subject of innumerable jests: it has given rise to popular proverbs in many countries . . . The superior readiness of speech of women is a concomitant of the fact that their vocabulary is smaller and more central than that of men.

[36] Ibid., p. 245. Elaborating on this characteristic (which he labels 'affectation'), Jespersen goes on to say at p. 246: 'There can be no doubt that women exercise a great and universal influence on linguistic development through their instinctive shrinking from coarse and gross expressions and their preference for refined and (in certain spheres) veiled and indirect expressions.'
[37] Ibid., p. 248.

But this again is connected with another indubitable fact, that women do not reach the same extreme points as men, but are nearer the average in most respects . . . Genius is more common among men by virtue of the same general tendency by which idiocy is more common among men. The two facts are but two aspects of a larger zoological fact – the greater variability of the male.[38]

And the causes for the major linguistic distinctions evinced between the sexes are:

mainly dependent on the division of labour enjoined in primitive tribes and to a great extent also among more civilized peoples. For thousands of years the work that especially fell to men was such as demanded an intense display of energy for a comparatively short period, mainly in war and in hunting. Here, however, there was not much occasion to talk, nay, in many circumstances talk might even be fraught with danger. And when that rough work was over, the man would either sleep or idle his time away, inert and torpid, more or less in silence. Woman on the other hand, had a number of domestic occupations which did not claim such an enormous output of spasmodic energy. To her was at first left not only agriculture, and a great deal of other work which in more peaceful times was taken over by men; but also much that has been till quite recently her almost exclusive concern – the care of children, cooking, brewing, baking, sewing, washing, etc. – things which for the most part demanded no deep thought, which were performed in company and could well be accompanied with a lively chatter.[39]

While it is easy enough to dismiss Jespersen out of hand for his subjective descriptions of women's language usage and domestic habits particularly in the light of more recent sociolinguistic theory, it is the case that his analyses, anecdotal as they may be, reflect commonly held beliefs about the way women use language – not only in 1922 when his book was published, but also in the present day. It is precisely because these folklinguistic myths about women's language have a millennia-old history, and are ubiquitous, that it is possible to ascertain Chaucer's own use of them in the depiction of, arguably, his greatest literary fiction, the Wife of Bath.

---

[38] Jespersen, *Language, Its Nature, Development, and Origin*, p. 253.
[39] Ibid., p. 254.

Man Writes Woman

If repetition, euphemism, hyperbole, unfinished sentences (and illogical-ity), limited vocabulary, volubility, and a contextual focus on domestic issues are characteristic of the deviant speech of women, and any indication of the limited nature of one's language, then certainly Alison is made a chief exemplar.[40] Throughout the *Prologue*, she is ventriloquised using hyperbole and phatic fillers: empty phrases such as 'by my fey' (line 203) and 'God woot' (used six times in a variety of combinations).[41] Such phrases are generally not only phatic, in that they add little to the semantic context, but they are, cumulatively, hyperbolic, giving an exaggerated effect to her various points. In its most positive interpretation, the Wife's apparent insistence on placing considerable emphasis on 'truth', and the witness of God's testimony in her text through the use of 'God woot', acts ironically to undermine the authority that she claims here for herself.

Hyperbole and the use of intensifying adverbs are well illustrated throughout the *Prologue*. I have already mentioned the use of 'God woot', but a different kind of hyperbole is yielded by the frequent use of the adverbs 'wel', 'ful', 'verray', 'so' (alone, 49 times) and 'ofte(n)'. These intensifiers are used throughout the *Prologue* – one hundred times, every eight lines or so, a percentage that is higher than other *Prologues*, such as that of the Pardoner (one every 15 lines), or the Miller (one every 10). The receptive consequences of using intensifiers in speech is to add to the exaggerative, emotive, and individuated nature of the discourse; judged against the 'norm' of language usage, the result is that the authority of the speaker is weakened. The following sample quotation from lines 27–30 illustrates this use of intensifiers (in the repetition and insistence on the truth of her personal knowledge in line 27, in particular):

> 'But wel I woot, expres, withoute lye,
> God bad us for to wexe and multiplye;
> That gentil text kan I wel understonde.
> Eek wel I woot, he seyde myn housbonde . . .'

[40] As a model of the non-standard, the ab-norm-al, deviating from the norm (the powerful male hegemony), the Wife is a fictional example of the powerless mode of discourse.
[41] The analysis of fillers is made more complex by the verse form, which by virtue of the couplets occasionally demands phatic phrases to complete the scansion and rhyme.

Alison is here made to emphasise the veracity of her experience, but in a manner that is less declarative and assertive than defensive and exaggerative. Chaucer's mimicry of the stereotypical features of a woman's speech, then, renders the content of that speech less authoritative, more subjective and less effective than it might otherwise have been.

From this brief survey, Chaucer's encapsulation of stereotypical aspects of women's speech pre-empts many of the same elements described in Jespersen's account of the variation between the sexes' use of language in his chapter. To these folklinguistic characteristics can be added others that have been proposed by more modern sociolinguists in the last few decades. Robin Lakoff, in *Language and Woman's Place*,[42] for example, asserts that adjectives such as 'adorable', 'charming', 'sweet', 'lovely', and 'divine' belong to women's speech. These adjectives are 'terms that denote approval of the trivial, the personal; that express approbation in terms of one's own personal emotional reaction, rather than by gauging the likely general reaction.'[43] In terms of syntax too, according to Lakoff, 'women's speech is peculiar'.[44] Women use tag-questions: 'used when the speaker is stating a claim, but lacks full confidence in the truth of that claim'.[45] Other characteristics would include the tendency of women to being open to interruption by men in mixed sex conversations.[46] Each of these so-called traits of women's language have been shown to be questionable, measured as they were against the norm of male 'standard' patterns of language usage.[47] These conclusions by Lakoff and other linguists have rightly been the focus of corrective criticism by subsequent empirical research, particularly because the conclusions drawn from these early observations was that women's language use was inferior to that of men: less assertive, less convincing, less credible.[48]

It is only the recent late twentieth-century corrective criticism of feminist linguists that has succeeded in beginning to reposition

[42] *Language and Woman's Place* (New York: Harper & Row, 1975), p. 226.
[43] Ibid., p. 227.
[44] Ibid., p. 228.
[45] Ibid., p. 229.
[46] For a critique of which see Spender, *Man Made Language*, pp. 43–5.
[47] See, for example, Spender, *Man Made Language*, pp. 8–9; Cameron, *Feminism and Linguistic Theory*, 33–4.
[48] Lakoff 'states that women lack authority and seriousness, they lack conviction and confidence. In her view, in comparison with the (ostensibly) forceful and effective language of men, women are tentative, hesitant, even trivial, and are therefore "deficient"': Spender, *Man Made Language*, p. 8.

women's speech as different from but equal to that of men. Thus Chaucer's fourteenth-century replication of stereotypical features of women's speech in his portrait of the Wife of Bath succeeds in producing – for him and for his contemporary audience – a fictional woman who is ultimately 'deficient' in her discourse in comparison to the norm of the male pilgrims. He fundamentally accomplishes the depiction of a woman who is undermined by her own prolixity and hyperbole, and who, furthermore, exhibits virtually all the major elements of women's stereotypical language usage in her *Prologue*.

In this respect, in addition to the features noted above, the Wife's discourse frequently demonstrates the use of tag questions, rhetorical questions, and questions that are answered intratextually – 39 times in all: when she tells her audience that she often went to vigils, processions and the like (lines 555–8), and wore her scarlet robes (559), 'Thise wormes, ne thise motthes, ne thise mytes, / Upon my peril, frete hem never a deel; / And wostow why? For they were used weel' (lines 560–2); or, again, 'What rekketh me', she says, 'thogh folk sete vileynye / Of shrewed Lameth and his bigamye?' (lines 53–4), showing here both colloquial language as well as rhetorical questioning, seeking approval or co-operation from her audience in the claim of her often-married status. In relation to the declamation by Jespersen[49] and others that women avoid language that directly pertains to taboo subjects such as sex or parts of the body, the Wife engages in euphemism, as well as underlining her point with a rhetorical question, ultimately seeking agreement from her audience:

> Of uryne, and oure bothe thynges smale
> Were eek to knowe a femele from a male,
> And for noon oother cause, – say ye no?
> The experience woot wel it is noght so.[50]

The number of such questions within this text[51] contrasts with one question in the *Pardoner's Prologue*, and one in the *Parson's Prologue*, each of them a shorter text than the *Wife's Prologue*; the proportional disparity is evident enough.

As regards interruption, the Wife of Bath is interrupted twice: once

---

[49] See above, page 107.
[50] *Wife's Prologue*, lines 121–4.
[51] The number of interrogative structures, whether rhetorical or direct, will, to an extent, depend on the editorial process. The majority of them are unequivocally provided by the syntax.

by the laudatory Pardoner at lines 163–92, and once by the Friar's laughter at line 829. The first of these interruptions is worth citing in context:

> Up stirte the pardoner, and that anon:
> 'Now, dame,' quod he, 'by God and by seint john!
> Ye been a noble prechour in this cas.
> I was aboute to wedde a wyf; allas!
> What sholde I bye it on my flessh so deere?
> Yet hadde I levere wedde no wyf to-yeere!'
> 'Abyde!' quod she, 'my tale is nat bigonne.
> Nay, thou shalt drynken of another tonne,
> Er that I go, shal savoure wors than ale.
> And whan that I have toold thee forth my tale
> Of tribulacion in mariage,
> Of which I am expert in al myn age,
> This is to seyn, myself have been the whippe, –
> Than maystow chese wheither thou wolt sippe
> Of thilke tonne that I shal abroche.
> Be war of it, er thou to ny approche;
> For I shal telle ensamples mo than ten.
> – Whoso that nyl be war by othere men,
> By hym shul othere men corrected be. –
> The same wordes writeth Ptholomee;
> Rede in his Almageste, and take it there.'
> 'Dame, I wolde praye yow, if youre wyl it were,'
> Seyde this pardoner, 'as ye bigan,
> . Telle forth youre tale, spareth for no man,
> And teche us yonge men of youre praktike.'
> 'Gladly', quod she, 'sith it may yow like;
> But that I praye to al this compaignye,
> If that I speke after my fantasye,
> As taketh not agrief of that I seye;
> For myn entente is nat but for to pleye.'[52]

In this particular excerpt, many of the facets of the stereotypical woman's language usage are exemplified. Not only is the Wife interrupted (albeit to be asked to give advice), but she does not hold her train of thought (demonstrating the lack of logicality or sequenced thought so often attributed to women); she cites authority to lend weight to her argument but attributes the proverb wrongly to Ptolemy;

---

[52] *Wife's Prologue*, lines 163–92.

and she exaggerates for effect in declaring that she will tell more than ten examples of, presumably, tribulation in marriage. While other pilgrims are interrupted – Chaucer the pilgrim, for example, in the telling of *The Tale of Sir Thopas* – and while other pilgrims use hyperbole, such as the Physician in his formulaic description of Virginia, for instance, it is the bringing together of all these features in the Wife of Bath's *Prologue* that marks her character out as employing, to a considerable extent, the stereotypical characteristics of women's speech labelled (until recently, that is) 'deficient' or 'deviant' in relation to the norm of male language usage. Through these characteristics, Chaucer effectually renders his literary creation 'powerless' in the face of masculine oppression: an oppression filtered through judgements about language use, reflecting and contributing to patriarchal social and cultural paradigms.

'Experience, though noon auctoritee' – the opening gambit of the Wife – is, then, precisely the point; she has no authority, either through her inability to read and interpret the authoritative texts she cites, or through her teaching and preaching in the manner Chaucer permits her. But any pretence at authority that Chaucer allows, and which is seized upon by positivist readings of the Wife, is undermined conclusively by Chaucer's stereotypical and perceptibly inferior forms of women's speech recorded and employed by him.

The emphasis on the Wife and her spoken language is most clearly pointed up by the semioclastic act in which she engages when she literally and deliberately destroys the written word contained in Jankyn's book. This act privileges metaphorically the Wife's reliance on the spoken word for authority as well as symbolising her derision of everything Jankyn's book represents. This foregrounding of the vocal, the supposed domain of women, extends to the gendered aspect of actual spoken discourse: that is that women are reliant on the uttered word – theirs primarily by virtue of exclusion from formal education – but that it can never be superior to, or more authoritative than, men's reliance on the written word, on traditional *auctoritee*.

Moreover, the Wife, in contrast to the other female tellers, is not 'literate': the level of traditional literacy she attains, she attains through hearing, not reading the Latin texts. Whereas the Prioress and Second Nun have access to (at the very least in the vernacular), and repeat, traditional tales in a manner very much according both with their positions and their stereotypical gendered roles, the Wife is ostensibly free of these ideologically imposed constraints. Although at times the Wife immerses herself in the discourse of patriarchy, presumably to be heard – to sound authoritative – she is ultimately unable to overcome this discourse[53] because of her verbal power-lessness: the way in which, through Chaucer, her words render the argument ineffectual.

Illustrating this most effectively is the analysis of that spoken word within the framework of sociolinguistics or, more appropriately, folklinguistics. It is here, within that analysis, that the nexus of her power is located, for it is here that Chaucer is operating at his most indefinable level: one might wonder what it is that he intended in ventriloquising so effectively the voice of the woman. Depending on how one interprets the text, the author has either created a female fiction whose power is defined by *what* she says,[54] or a female fiction who becomes powerless through the manner in which she speaks, no matter what she actually says.

Chaucer's awareness of language usage and the power of language is everywhere evident. He creates an opaque text through his multi-layered approach, breaking many of the rules of conversation between reader and writer that demand clarity of meaning, a process of implicature where the relationship between what is stated and what is implicit is clear, and where there is explicit co-operation. The lack of explicitness in the creation of the Wife has led inevitably to the problematising of what she is meant to stand for, and what Chaucer intended through her depiction. She has been labelled as the worst of women, as a proto-feminist, appropriated by scholars to meet their own requirements. The same, of course, is true of Chaucer. What is certain is that as author he questions issues of language and power, of typical fourteenth-century gender roles and social relationships in a way that is itself didactic. Ironically, perhaps, the ultimate powerlessness of the female voice is that, in reality, it does not exist, for this is not a woman speaking here giving voice to the concerns of female experience, it is a male author enacting the role of woman, silencing her as effectively as the female audience of texts such as *Hali Meiðhad* and *Ancrene Wisse* are silenced.[55]

---

[53] A point made by Morrison in 'Don't Ask, Don't Tell: The Wife of Bath and Vernacular Translations', pp. 122–23.

[54] Which would be Carruthers' reading in 'The Wife of Bath and the Painting of Lions'.

[55] In both these earlier texts, the authors imagine their audiences' responses and questions in a series of indirectly reported questions framed by 'You ask . . .', and in rhetorical questions seeking the audiences' approbation. See B. Millett and J. Wogan-Browne, ed., *Medieval English Prose for Women from the Katherine Group and 'Ancrene Wisse'* (Oxford: Oxford University Press, 1992).

Chaucer has the opportunity to subvert social expectation, to undermine stereotype, but it is not an opportunity he exploits here, though he may appear to be doing so at the surface level. On the contrary, as a man of his day, he confirms the stereotypes of women, but also indirectly raises issues about the validity of ideological norms that he subsequently refuses to clarify. No matter how much or how little Chaucer and subsequent critics sympathise with the character of the Wife of Bath, may celebrate her creation as a wonderfully independent, free-thinking woman or might condemn her as the harridan of the anti-feminist diatribes she so joyously appropriates, she is ultimately powerless: powerless not so much through what she says, but through *how* she says it. And that makes her a fourteenth-century victim of patriarchal ideology, no matter what our own view of her might be.

In the *Envoy to Bukton*, the Wife is presented as a humorous case study against the recipient's imminent marriage, and against women like her in general.[56] While we may be meant to laugh at her, even find her a joyous and exuberant creation, she is, in the final analysis, a stereotype. It is precisely because Chaucer adopts, with considerable success, the stratagem of replicating women's speech that critics and students are so frequently momentarily beguiled into believing they are reading the real words of a real woman. Chaucer's linguistic acuity and his ability to deceive – despite the formal restraints of the written verse form – are what make his observations, not only of social *mores* and culture in late fourteenth-century England, but also of social and communicative interaction so interesting. Aspects of gendered language use are brought to the fore in the Wife's *Prologue* that would not be the focus of sustained scholarly research for another five hundred years, and in this, as in so many other things, Chaucer's innovation is remarkable.[57]

---

[56]   This lytel writ, proverbes, or figure
       I sende yow; take kepe of yt, I rede;
       Unwys is he that kan no wele endure.
       If thou be siker, put the nat in drede.
       The Wyf of Bathe I pray yow that ye rede
       Of this matere that we have on honde.
       God graunte yow your lyf frely to lede
       In fredam, for ful hard is to be bonde.

Lenvoy de Chaucer a Bukton, in the *Riverside Chaucer*, pp. 655–6, lines 25–32.
[57] I should like to thank Professors Greg Walker, David F. Johnson and Roy M. Liuzza for their helpful comments on an early draft of this paper.

'Cursed folk of Herodes al new': Supersessionist Typology and Chaucer's Prioress

ANNE MARIE D'ARCY

Tell me this. If a man were to have slain your son, would you endure to look upon him, or accept his greeting? Would you not shun him as a wicked demon, as the devil himself? They slew the Son of your Lord: do you have the boldness to enter with them under the same roof?[1]

FOR US, LIVING IN the sulphuric wake of the *Shoah*, our attention is ineluctably drawn toward the pervasive anti-Judaism of *The Prioress's Tale*. As this aspect of the narrative strikes us as abhorrent, it remains difficult to approach objectively the primary, edifying purpose of this *Tale*. As Alexander points out: 'One may acknowledge the aesthetic power of a piece of writing without endorsing its sentiments.'[2] However, it is important to note that the *Tale* merely reflects the inimical typification of the Jewish people as evil personified, which, although 'implicit in the medieval point of view',[3] was radicated in the prejudices of the classical period, came to fruition in patristic *adversus Judaeos* polemic, and gained fresh racial impetus in the last two centuries, with the most pernicious of consequences. Indeed, that this accretive process of dehuminisation was exploited by the ideologues of the Third Reich 'cannot be discounted, despite the adoption of a secular racial myth of anti-semitism for the earlier religious myth'.[4]

---

[1] John Chrysostom, *Eight Homilies Against the Jews*, 1, 7, PG 48, 854. *See Discourses Against Judaizing Christians*, trans. P. W. Harkins (Washington: Catholic University of America, 1979), p. 28.

[2] P. S. Alexander, 'Madame Eglentyne, Geoffrey Chaucer and the Problem of Medieval Anti-Semitism', *Bulletin of the John Rylands Library* 74 (1992), 109–20 (at p. 120).

[3] J. Trachtenberg, *The Devil and the Jews: The Medieval Conception of the Jew and Its Relation to Modern Antisemitism* (New Haven, CT: Yale University Press, 1943), p. 22.

[4] R. R. Ruether, 'Anti-Semitisim in Christian Theology', *Theology Today* 30 (1974), 365–81 (at p. 381). On this point see also Alexander, 'Madame Eglentyne', p. 111: 'What we have in Chaucer may be anti-Judaism (and deplorable), but not anti-Semitism in any exact sense. The dissimilarities can,

Refracted through the prismatic response to the full horror of the *Shoah*, the anti-Judaism of the Prioress and her *Tale* has been the topic of considerable critical controversy.[5] Earlier generations of critics have tended to concur that the portrait of the Prioress in the *General Prologue* pokes gentle fun at her worldliness and courtly affectations: 'The rippling undercurrent of satire is always there; but it is Chaucer's own peculiar satire', as Power puts it, 'mellow, amused, uncondemning, the most subtle kind of satire, which does not depend upon exaggeration.'[6] Similarly, Robertson sees a level of 'urbane sarcasm, or *astysmos*', that is, 'sarcasm without bitterness'.[7] However, in their efforts to absolve the author from any taint of anti-Judaism, several critics have not only interpreted the portrait as a caustic indictment of the Prioress's true nature, but also see this condemnatory stance reflected in the *Tale*. This strain of criticism, which accuses the Prioress specifically of anti-semitism, was initiated by Schoeck's pivotal article, published in 1956.[8] As Collette points out, these attempts to create a sense of *Verfremdung* between the character and her author presumes

---

however, be overplayed. The fact is that mediaeval Christendom espoused a set of beliefs which are strikingly congruent in content and structure with the nineteenth-century anti-Semitic creed.'

[5] Cf. Alexander, 'Madame Eglentyne', p. 109: 'Critics cannot view the Tale after the holocaust in quite the same way as they viewed it before. Since the holocaust anti-Semitism has become academically discredited: it is now one of the few generally acknowledged intellectual heresies. So for a critic today to expound the Tale and to ignore the question of anti-Semitism would strike most educated people as displaying a detachment from life bordering on the irresponsible, if not the perverse.'

[6] E. Power, *Medieval People* (London: Methuen, 1924; repr. 1986), p. 74.

[7] D. W. Robertson Jr, *A Preface to Chaucer: Studies in Medieval Perspectives* (Princeton: Princeton University Press, 1962), pp. 244, 288. Robertson does, however, acknowledge that the tone 'becomes somewhat more bitter and sarcastic' at *General Prologue*, I. 142, *The Riverside Chaucer*, ed. L. D. Benson et al. (Oxford: Oxford University Press, 1987), p. 25.

[8] R. J. Schoeck, 'Chaucer's Prioress: Mercy and Tender Heart', *The Bridge: A Yearbook of Judaeo-Christian Studies* 2 (New York, 1956), 245–58, repr. in *Chaucer Criticism: The Canterbury Tales I*, ed. by R. J. Schoeck and J. Taylor (Notre Dame, IN: University of Indiana Press, 1960), pp. 239–55. See also E. Talbot Donaldson, *Chaucer's Poetry* (New York: Ronald Press, 1958); P. F. Baum, *Chaucer: A Critical Appreciation* (Durham, NC: Duke University Press, 1958); R. Preston, 'Chaucer, His Prioress, the Jews, and Professor Robinson', *Notes and Queries* 106 (1961), 7–8; A. T. Gaylord, 'The Unconquered Tale of the Prioress', *Papers of the Michigan Academy of Science, Arts, and Letters* 47 (1962), 613–31; M. Cohen, 'Chaucer's Prioress and Her Tale: A Study of Anal Character and Anti-Semitism', *Psychoanalytic Quarterly* 31 (1962), 232–49.

on Chaucer's part 'a disapproving distance from the Prioress and a social criticism that condemns the putative blindness of his own age'.[9] However, this position is undermined by the words of that most exemplary of pilgrims, the Parson, whom Friedman rightly describes as 'the one religious in the pilgrimage who approximates Chaucer's ideal of the perfect man of God'.[10] In his equation of the 'cursede Jewes' with 'the devel',[11] the Parson mirrors the Prioress's hackneyed, postilic identification of *Populus Israel* with 'Oure firste foo',[12] that is, '*serpens antiquus qui vocatur Diabolus et Satanas*'.[13]

Moreover, the implacable, atavistic sliver of *duritia* that the Prioress carries for the Jews in her paradoxically 'tendre herte'[14] is worth comparing to the Man of Law's adamantine response to the heathen Saracens.[15] He describes the Sultana in terms that are forcibly reminiscent of the imagery deployed by the Prioress and the Parson *contra Judeos*: she is the 'welle of vices', and the 'roote of iniquitee', and he goes on to castigate her as a 'serpent under femynyntee, / Lik to the serpent depe in helle ybounde!'[16] This not only recalls the traditional strain of anti-feminist figurative description that associates women with Satan as the Edenic serpent with a female head, but also an offshoot of this iconographic commonplace whereby Synagoga is represented in terms reminiscent

---

[9] C. Collette, 'Critical Approaches to the *Prioress's Tale* and the *Second Nun's Tale*', in *Chaucer's Religious Tales*, ed. C. D. Benson and E. Robertson (Cambridge: D. S. Brewer, 1990), pp. 95–107 (at 98).

[10] A. B. Friedman, 'The *Prioress's Tale* and Chaucer's Anti-Semitism', *Chaucer Review* 9 (1974), 118–29 (at p. 123).

[11] *Parson's Tale*, X. 599, *Riverside Chaucer*, p. 307.

[12] *Prioress's Tale*, VII. 558, ibid., p. 212. Cf. 570; 574; 599; 631; 685, ibid., pp. 210–12.

[13] Revelations 12. 9: 'that old serpent, who is called the devil and Satan'. All Bible quotations in Latin are taken from *Biblia sacra iuxta vulgatam versionem*, ed. R. Weber *et al.*, 3rd ed. (Stuttgart, 1983). All Bible quotations in English are taken from the Douay-Rheims translation of the Vulgate, with notes by Bishop Challoner.

[14] *General Prologue*, I. 150, *Riverside Chaucer*, p. 25.

[15] As F. H. Ridley, ibid., p. 913, points out. See also G. Dharmaraj, 'Multicultural Subjectivity in Reading Chaucer's *Man of Law's Tale*', *Medieval Feminist Newsletter* 16 (1993), pp. 4–7; S. Delany, *The Naked Text: Chaucer's Legend of Good Women* (Berkeley, Los Angeles and London: University of California Press, 1994), pp. 164–86, esp. 177–9; S. Schibanoff, 'Worlds Apart: Orientalism, Antifeminism, and Heresy in Chaucer's *Man of Law's Tale*', *Exemplaria* 8 (1996), 59–96.

[16] *Man of Law's Tale*, II. 323; 358; 360–1, *Riverside Chaucer*, p. 92.

of this therianthropic, female personification.[17] That this typology is projected on to Jew and Saracen alike is hardly surprising. Indeed, as Trachtenberg points out, Judaism was frequently 'regarded not merely as one with Christian schismatics but as the ally of the Moorish and later of the Turkish hosts'.[18] The belief that Jews were synonymous with Saracens is found as early as the ninth-century polemicist, Agobard of Lyons,[19] and we find this idea gaining fresh impetus in Western Europe as a result of the 1321 Leper Plot.[20] In France, notably at Chinon and Vitry, a pogrom ensued in the wake of this putative international conspiracy on the part of lepers, Jews and Muslims to poison not only the wells of France and Navarre, but 'all kingdoms subject to Christ's faith'.[21] The yoking of Jews and Saracens as heretics is also found in the *consilia* of one of the most distinguished canonists associated with the Rota at Avignon, Oldradus de Ponte, who died sometime after 1335.[22] Moreover, the

[17] See A. M. D'Arcy, '*Li Anemis Meismes*: Satan and Synagogue in *La Queste del Saint Graal*', *Medium Ævum* 66 (1997), 207–35 (at pp. 207–13), which provides a summary of scholarship in relation to the anti-Judaic context.

[18] Trachtenberg, *Devil and the Jews*, p. 183. Cf. also the controversial argument set forth in A. H. Cutler and H. E. Cutler, *The Jew as Ally of the Muslim: Medieval Roots of Anti-Semitism* (Notre Dame, IN: University of Indiana Press, 1986).

[19] *De Judaicis superstitionibus*, 21, *PL* 104, 95–6; CCCM 52, 215–16. See also F. Wiegrand, 'Agobard von Lyon und die Judenfrage', in *Festschrift dem Prinzregenten Luitpold von Bayern zum 80. Geburtstage dargebracht von der Univ. Erlangen* (Erlangen and Leipzig, 1901), pp. 3–32, esp. 11; Mgr. Bressoles, *Doctrine et action politique d'Agobard I, Saint Agobard, évêque de Lyon*, L'Eglise et l'état au moyen âge IX (Paris, 1949), pp. 101–19; A. Cabaniss, *Agobard of Lyons: Churchman and Critic* (Syracuse, NY, 1953); B. Blumenkranz, 'Deux compilations canoniques de Florus de Lyon et l'action antijuive d'Agobard', *Revue historique de droit français et étranger*, 4th ser., 33 (1955), 227–54, 560–82; K. Stow, 'Agobard of Lyon and the Origins of the Medieval Conception of the Jew', *Conservative Judaism* 29 (1974), 56–65.

[20] See Trachtenberg, *Devil and the Jews*, pp. 100–8; V. R. Rivière Chalan, *La Marque infâme des lépreux et des christians sous l'Ancien Régime: des cours des miracles aux cagoteries* (Paris: La Pensée Universelle, 1978); M. C. Barber, 'Lepers, Jews and Moslems: The Plot to Overthrow Christendom in 1321', *History* 66 (1981), 1–17; E. A. R. Brown, 'Philip V, Charles IV, and the Jews of France: The Alleged Expulsion of 1322', *Speculum* 66 (1991), 294–329, esp. 301–5.

[21] See H. Duplès-Agier, 'Choix de pièces inédites . . . XIV: Ordonnance de Philippe le Long contre les lépreux (21 juin 1321)', *Bibliothèque de l'Ecole des chartes*, 4th ser., 3 (1857), 265–72 (at p. 270): 'sed etiam universorum regnorum Christi fidei subjectorum'; trans. Brown, 'Philip V, Charles IV, and the Jews', p. 301.

[22] W. Stalls, 'Jewish Conversion to Islam: The Perspective of a *Quaestio*', *Revista*

association persists in the *adversus Judaeos* tract incorporated into the labyrinthine *Summa de Quaestionibus Armenorum* of Richard Fitzralph.[23] Thus it seems likely that the treatment *de Judaeis et Saracenis* in Chaucer reflects an attitude still prevalent in the fourteenth century, whereby the *disparitas cultus* represented by both groups, whether defined as infidels or as heretics,[24] was

española de Teologia 43 (1983), 235–51; N. Zacour, *Jews and Saracens in the Consilia of Oldradus de Ponte*, Pontifical Institute Studies and Texts 100 (Toronto: Toronto University Press, 1990). See also T. Schmidt, 'Die Konsilien des Oldrado da Ponte als Geschichtsquelle', *Consilia im späten Mittelalter: Zum historischen Aussagewert einer Quellengattung*, ed. I. Baumgärtner, Studi: Studienreihe des Deutschen Studienzentrums in Venedig 13 (Sigmaringen: 1995), 53–64. Oldradus is generally thought to have died in 1335, but according to the English canonist, Thomas Fastolf, he was active in the Rota in 1336 or 1337; cf. Zacour, *Jews and Saracens*, p. 7; B. McManus, 'The *Consilia* and *Quaestiones* of Oldradus de Ponte', *Bulletin of Medieval Canon Law*, ns 23 (1999), 71–93, esp. 85, 102.

[23] On this point see B. Blumenkranz, 'Anti-Jewish Polemics and Legislation in the Middle Ages: Literary Fiction or Reality?', *Journal of Jewish Studies* 15 (1964), 125–140, esp. 134–5; N. Daniel, *Islam and the West: The Making of an Image*, rev. ed. (Oxford: Clarendon Press, 1993), p. 214: 'Fitzralph, after his consideration of the Qur'án, in his eighteenth book, went on to consider the damnation of the Jews during the Apostolic Age in the book following. Talmud and Qur'án might be paired as sources of error.' See also K. Walsh, *A Fourteenth-Century Scholar and Primate: Richard FitzRalph in Oxford, Avignon and Armagh* (Oxford: Oxford University Press, 1981), esp. pp. 129–81; A. K. Walsh, 'Zwischen Mission und Dialog. Zu den Bemühungen um Aussöhnung mit den Ostkirchen im Vorfeld des Konzils von Ferrara-Florenz', in *Toleranz im Mittelalter*, ed. A. Patschovsky and H. Zimmermann (Sigmaringen: Thorbecke, 1998), pp. 297–333, esp. 304–322.

[24] Schibanoff, 'Worlds Apart', pp. 70–1, rightly draws attention to the distinction in canon law between pagan, infidel and heretic, but as far as polemic and its influence on the arts is concerned, this distinction would appear to be a great deal more nebulous; cf. J. A. Hoeppner Moran Cruz, 'Popular Attitudes Toward Islam in Medieval Europe', in *Western Views of Islam in Medieval and Early Modern Europe*, ed. D. R. Blanks and M. Frassetto (Basingstoke: Macmillan, 1999), pp. 55–81, which provides a re-evaluation of B. P. Edmonds, 'Le Portrait des Sarrasins dans *La Chanson de Roland*', *French Review* 44 (1971), 870–8, and N. Daniel, *Heroes and Saracens: An Interpretation of the Chansons de Geste* (Edinburgh: Edinburgh University Press, 1984), pp. 121–78. On the Jews as heretics, see Trachtenberg, *Devil and the Jews*, pp. 170–87; R. Manselli, 'La Polémique contre les Juifs dans la polémique antihérétique', in *Juifs et judaïsme de Languedoc*, Les Cahiers de Fanjeaux 12 (Toulouse: Privat, 1977), 251–67. On Islam as a heresy see M. T. d'Alverny, 'La Connaissance de l'Islam en Occident du IXe au milieu du XIIe siècle', in *L'Occidente e l'Islam nell'Alto Medioevo*, Settimana di Studio del Centro Italiano di Studi sull'Alto Medioevo 12 (Spoleto, 1965), pp. 572–602; Daniel, *Islam and the West*, pp. 186–219.

viewed in terms of a pernicious, inimical syzygy which posed an unremitting threat to Christian orthodoxy.

Thus, *The Prioress's Tale* is as serious in intent as that of the Parson or the Man of Law, but the tone emphasises the pathetic, rather than the penitential or providential. It has been pointed out by several critics that the pathetic timbre of such *Tales* as those of the Prioress and the Man of Law is perhaps more alienating to modern sensibilities than any other aspect of *The Canterbury Tales*.[25] Chaucer strives to elicit a wrenching, albeit artistically satisfying, sense of *empatheia*, rather than a wry parody of cloying, mawkish sentimentality which carries an implicit, detached criticism of the tellers and their Tales. In particular, *The Prioress's Tale* reflects 'the late fourteenth-century shift in sensibility, which, following the so-called triumph of nominalism, produced the flowering of English mysticism, a highly particularized, emotional style in the arts, and the ascendancy of the heart over the reason in religious matters'.[26] This compunctious insistence that the head must cede spiritual dominion to the heart finds poignant expression in the visual arts, as the hieratic concept of the *Rex gloriae* as cosmic Redeemer 'came to be replaced by the heart-rending image of the Broken Body, now ineffably mild and sad, now grim to the point of gruesomeness'.[27] We may note the widespread popularity of the motif of the naked, suffering God-man, variously known as *Imago pietatis*, the *Erbärmdebild*, the *Schmerzensmann*, the *Pathétique*, or the Man of Sorrows.[28] In the related motif of the *Marienklage*, *Vesperbild*, or

[25] See in particular, R. W. Frank Jr, 'Pathos in Chaucer's Religious Tales', in *Chaucer's Religious Tales*, ed. C. D. Benson and E. Robertson (Cambridge: D. S. Brewer, 1990), pp. 39–52 (at 36).

[26] C. P. Collette, 'Sense and Sensibility in the Prioress's Tale', *Chaucer Review* 15 (1981), 138–50 (at p. 138); cf. D. Knowles, *The Evolution of Medieval Thought* (London: Longman, 1962), p. 332.

[27] E. Panofsky, *Early Netherlandish Painting: Its Origins and Its Character*, 2 vols (Cambridge, Mass.: Harvard University Press, 1958), I, 73.

[28] See E. Panofsky, '*Imago Pietatis*, Ein Beitrag zur Typengeschichte des "Schmerzensmanns" und der "Maria Mediatrix"', in *Festschrift für Max J. Friedländer zum 60. Geburtstage* (Leipzig, 1927), pp. 261–308; G. von der Osten, *Der Schmerzensmann, Typengeschichte eines deutschen Andachtsbildwerkes von 1300 bis 1600* (Berlin, 1935); C. Bertelli, 'The *Image of Pity* in Santa Croce in Gerusalemme', in *Essays in the History of Art Presented to Rudolf Wittkower*, ed. D. Fraser, H. Hibbard and M. J. Lewine (London: Phaidon, 1967), pp. 40–55; C. Eisler, 'The Golden Christ of Cortona and the Man of Sorrows in Italy', *Art Bulletin* 51 (1969), 107–18, 233–46; G. Schiller, *Iconography of Christian Art*, trans. J. Seligman, 2 vols (London: Lund Humphries, 1971), II, 119–229; H. Belting, 'An Image and Its Function in the Liturgy: The Man of Sorrows in

Pietà,[29] Mary either clutches 'the body of her Son as if unable to relinquish Him to the tomb, or dreaming that she held Him in her lap once more as an infant'.[30] This image of the all too human Broken Body, mourned by the swooning, piteous mother, sometimes flanked by her Son's closest companions, is designed to elicit an empathetic response, whether the medium is painting, sculpture, devotional meditations, mystical treatises, or the Middle English religious lyric.[31] The Prioress's emphasis on the suffering of the 'litel clergeon', done to death by the demonic Jews in an eldritch *imitatio Christi*, is carefully designed to elicit similar feelings of empathy, and the conclusion of her *Tale* is curiously reminiscent of the *pathos* gestures characteristic of the *Pietà* motif.

However, as Nolan points out,[32] the imagery of the *Prologue* is

Byzantium', *Dumbarton Oaks Papers* 34–5 (1980–1), 1–16; E. Mâle, *Religious Art in France, the Late Middle Ages: A Study of Medieval Iconography and Its Sources*, ed. H. Bober, trans. M. Mathews (Princeton: Princeton University Press, 1984), pp. 94–100, esp. 94–7, 470–2nn.

[29] On this point see W. Pinder, 'Die dichterische Wurzel der Pietà', *Repertorium für Kunstwissenschaft* 42 (1920), 144–63; G. Lill, 'Die früheste deutsche Vespergruppe', *Der Cicerone* 14 (1924), 660–2; W. Passarge, *Das deutsche Vesperbild im Mittelalter* (Cologne: Marcan, 1924); G. Swarzenski, 'Italienische Quellen der deutschen Pietà', in *Festschrift Heinrich Welfflin. Beiträge zur Kunst und Geistesgeschichte zum 21. Juni 1924, überreicht von Freunden und Schülern* (Munich, 1924), 127–34; K. Künstle, *Ikonographie der christlichen Kunst*, 2 vols (Freiburg im Breisgau: Herder, 1928), I. 484–9; W. Kerte, 'Deutsche Vesperbilder in Italien', *Kunstgeschichtliches Jahrbuch der Bibliotheca Hertziana* 1 (Leipzig, 1937), 1–38; E. Reiners-Ernst, *Das freudvolle Vesperbild und die Anfänge der Pietàvorstellung* (Munich: Filser, 1939); C. Gravenkamp, *Marienklage. das deutsche Vesperbild im vierzehnten und im frühen fünfsehnten Jahrhundert* (Aschaffenburg: Pattloch, 1948); P. Bloch, 'Die Pietà Schnütgen, in *Mouseion: Studien aus Kunst und Geschichte für Otto H. Förster*, ed. H. Ladendorf (Cologne: Dumont, 1960), pp. 211–14; T. Dobrzeniecki, 'Mediaeval Sources of the Pietà', *Bulletin du Musée National de Varsovie* 8 (1967), 5–24; W. Krönig, *Rheinische Vesperbilder* (Mönchengladbach: Kühlen, 1967); P. Hawel, *Die Pietà: Eine Blüte der Kunst* (Würzburg: Echter, 1985); W. H. Forsyth, *The Pietà in French Later Gothic Sculpture: Regional Variations* (New York: Metropolitan Museum of Art, 1995). For a good discussion of the theological background see S. Ringbom, *Icon to Narrative: The Rise of the Dramatic Close-Up in Fifteenth-Century Devotional Painting*, 2nd ed. (Doornspijk: Davaco, 1984), pp. 11–71.

[30] D. Denny, 'Notes on the Avignon Pietà', *Speculum* 44 (1969), 213–33 (at p. 213).

[31] Cf. *The Book of Margery Kempe*, ed. S. B. Meech and H. E. Allen, Early English Text Society, Original Series 212 (London, 1940; repr. London, 1961), p. 148.

[32] B. Nolan, 'Chaucer's Tales of Transcendence: Rhyme Royal and Christian Prayer in the Canterbury Tales', in *Chaucer's Religious Tales*, ed. C. D. Benson and E. Robertson (Cambridge: D. S. Brewer, 1990), pp. 21–38 (at p. 35). For

eminently conventional, and employs several of the stock paradoxes
emblematic of Mariological typology. Mary is described as 'the white
lylye flour', and although the figure of the lily is polysemous,[33] the *lilium
inter spinas* of Song of Songs 2. 1–2 was interpreted as a figure both of
her fertility and perpetual virginity as 'a mayde alway'.[34] She is lauded
as 'the roote / Of bountee', which suggests her role as the *radix sancta*,
the holy root of salvation who made the Incarnation and therefore the
Redemption possible.[35] The divine paradox of her maternal yet virginal
state is celebrated in line 467, 'O mooder Mayde, O mayde Mooder
free!', which recalls Bernard of Clairvaux's use of liturgical antithesis in
the last canto of the *Paradiso*, 'Vergine madre, figlia del tuo Figlio'.[36]
The Prioress also refers to the idea that the plan of salvation depended
on Mary's voluntary decision at the Annunciation and emphasises her
humility in acquiescing to the Incarnation:

> O bussh unbrent, brennynge in Moyses sighte,
> That ravyshedest doun fro the deitee,
> Thurgh thyn humblesse, the Goost that in th'alighte.[37]

In praising the Virgin's '"humblesse" as the paradoxical source of her
power in becoming the human vessel of divine "sapience"',[38] the
Prioress subtly establishes herself in *imitatione Mariae*.[39] In disavowing

the sources of the *Prologue* see the summary of scholarship in *The Prioress's Tale*,
ed. B. Boyd, *A Variorum Edition of the Works of Geoffrey Chaucer*, vol. 2, part 20
(Norman, OK, and London, 1987), 4–8.
[33] E. Mâle, *Religious Art in France, the Thirteenth Century: A Study of Medieval
Iconography and Its Sources*, ed. H. Bober, trans. M. Mathews (Princeton, 1984),
p. 36: 'the lily sometimes signifies the Saviour, sometimes the saints, sometimes
the brilliance of the heavenly home, sometimes chastity'.
[34] *Prioress's Tale*, VII. 461–2, *Riverside Chaucer*, p. 209.
[35] Ibid., 465–6. The image is ultimately derived from Tertullian's exegesis of
Isaiah 11. 1, *De carne Christi*, 21, 5, CCSL 2, 911–12.
[36] Dante Alighieri, *Paradiso*, XXXIII, 1, *The Divine Comedy of Dante Alighieri
III: Paradiso*, trans. J. D. Sinclair, rev. ed. (Oxford, 1961), pp. 478–9: 'Virgin
Mother, daughter of your Son'. Cf. *Man of Law's Tale*, II. 841, *Riverside Chaucer*,
p. 99.
[37] *Prioress's Tale*, II. 457–60, ibid., p. 209. The image of Mary as the 'bussh
unbrent' is a traditional figure of her perpetual virginity; the bush which Moses
saw burning with fire in Exodus 3. 2, but not consumed; cf. 'An ABC', 89–7,
ibid., pp. 638–9.
[38] Nolan, 'Chaucer's Tales of Transcendence', p. 35.
[39] The *De imitatione Mariae* would seem to have gained currency through the
influential *Vita Christi* of the Carthusian theologian, Ludolf of Saxony (d. 1378);
cf. *Vita Jesu Christi*, 4. 2, 65, 4 vols (Paris, 1878), IV, esp. 143–5. On this point

her own 'konnyng' as almost too 'wayk' to rise to her sacrifice of
praise,[40] unless she is helped by Mary to bring forth the fruit of her lips in
her 'reverence',[41] she paradoxically asserts her own authority, which
mirrors that of the humble *Ancilla Dei* who is also the lachrymose *Mater
Dolorosa*, in whom the Church subsisted after the death of her Son.[42] As
Robertson points out, it is the Prioress's 'extreme humility', or at least
her adoption of the *humilitas* topos, which 'is in fact a crucial aspect of
her claim to authority as a religious speaker'.[43] In keeping with the
paradoxical nature of spiritual perfection and strength, this sacrifice of
praise is as that which issues from the lips of babes. As several critics
have noted, the introit, as it were, of the *Prologue* is a paraphrase of
matins in the *Officium Parvum* of the Virgin: 'O Lord, oure Lord, thy
name how merveillous / Is in this large world ysprad.'[44] These lines are
taken from Psalm 8: 'Out of mouth of infants and of sucklings thou hast

see Denny, 'Avignon Pietà', pp. 232–3. See also W. Baier, *Untersuchungen zu
den Passionbetrachtungen in der Vita Christi des Ludolf von Sachsen*, Analecta
Cartusiana 44 1–3 (Salzburg, 1977).
[40] Cf. Hebrews 13. 15. Cf. S. Hawkins, 'Chaucer's Prioress and the Sacrifice of
Praise', *Journal of English and Germanic Philology* 63 (1964), 599–624, esp. 620.
[41] *Prioress's Tale*, ll. 473, 481, *Riverside Chaucer*, p. 209.
[42] *Prioress's Tale*, ll. 457–60, ibid., p. 209. Although the tearful mother
characteristic of the Eastern *Staurotheotokia* was rejected by Ambrose in his
oft-quoted comment: 'Durum quidem funus videtis, sed stabat et sancta Maria
juxta crucem filii, et spectabat virgo sui unigeniti passionem. Stantem illam
lego, flentem non lego' (*De obitu Valentiniani consolatio*, 39, CSEL 73, 348), the
motif became increasingly common in the West during the later Middle Ages.
However, the Ambrosian emphasis on the paradoxical strength and authority
of Mary, by way of contrast to the absconding apostles, gained fresh
ecclesiological impetus during the fourteenth century, when some theologians,
most notably William of Ockham, Nicholas of Clémanges, and Conrad of
Gelnhausen, interpreted the belief that faith abided in Mary alone after the
death of Christ as testimony to the fact that the true Church may survive in a
single soul if the fabric of the institutionalised Church is rent and corrupted,
and thus insupportable. See Y. Congar, 'Incidence ecclésiologique d'un thème
de dévotion mariale', *Mélanges de science religieuse* 5 (1950), 277–92, esp. 286,
n. 1, who cites William of Ockham, *Dialogus*, 2, 25; cf. also 4, 12; 5, 101; 7, 47.
As Denny, 'Avignon Pietà', p. 215, points out: 'It is understandable that this
concept retained an appeal for many throughout the time of western schism
and the Conciliar Movement, a period of individual soul-searching and the
testing of allegiances. It offered a clear solution to problems of conscience
raised by a divided and partly discredited Church.'
[43] E. Robertson, 'Aspects of Female Piety in the *Prioress's Tale*', in *Chaucer's
Religious Tales*, ed. C. D. Benson and E. Robertson, pp. 145–60 (at p. 151).
[44] *Prioress's Tale*, ll. 453–4, *Riverside Chaucer*, p. 209. Cf. Hawkins, 'Chaucer's
Prioress', p. 605.

perfected praise.' Because 'praise' literally means 'strength' in this context, this verse was commonly taken to mean that the power of the Lord is paradoxically magnified because of the seemingly powerless instruments he chooses to confound the enemies of God: those who cannot usually express themselves in words, or indeed, by the Prioress's implication, 'wayk' women.[45] This mental association between *vox feminae* and mewling infants becomes readily apparent when she equates herself with 'a child of twelf month oold, or lesse, / 'that kan unnethes any word expresse', unless Mary guides her 'song'.[46]

The paraphrases of the *Officium* and *Officium Parvum* of the Virgin found in the *Prologue*, coupled with the allusions to Childermas according to Sarum Use, not only remind us of the Prioress's recital of the *officium divinum*, 'entuned' in a pronounced nasal drawl,[47] but, as generations of critics have noted, the typological significance of the *sancti innocentes*, found in Matthew 2: 16, is imbued with a fathomless resonance, given the cautionary tales of 'Children an heep, ycomen of Cristen blood' that underpin the *figura* of the clergeon.[48] Thus, her identification with infants and sucklings have led to the diagnosis of arrested development; or of an infantilism that causes her to behave 'as an emotional child "getting back" at the grown-up world which has injured her, but of which she has very little experience beyond her sense of injury'.[49] It could be argued with Friedman that her empathetic

---

[45] Cf. Robertson, 'Aspects of Female Piety', p. 153: 'The Prioress here reminds us that children have the authority to speak despite the fact that men usually are the "performers" of praise.' For an alternative reading, which addresses Hawkins' analysis of the Augustinian exegesis of Psalm 8 whereby infants and sucklings represent the first stage of spiritual understanding ('Chaucer's Prioress', p. 605); cf. L. O. Fradenburg, 'Criticism, Anti-Semitism, and the Prioress's Tale', *Exemplaria* 1 (1989), 69–115 (at pp. 91–2): 'the Prioress actually collapses the maturational narrative understanding proposed in Augustine's commentary, by *paralleling* the "mouth of children" with "men of dignitee". Levelling in this instance becomes a way of collapsing even the speech of powerful men into the "soukynge" of the "mouth of children", of collapsing vocal distance from the body back into the relation of mouth to the breast.' Cf. also Augustine, *Enarratio in psalmo VIII*, 5–6, CCSL 39, 50–2.

[46] *Prioress's Tale*, ll. 485–7, *Riverside Chaucer*, p. 209.

[47] *General Prologue*, l. 122–3, ibid., p. 25.

[48] Alexander, 'Madam Eglentyne', p. 112, remarks that it is 'chilling' to find this reference in the introductory stage of the Tale: 'Why "blood"? Was Chaucer strapped for a rhyme for "stood", or is there a more sinister note here? Is Christian blood any different from Jewish blood?'

[49] R. P. Tripp, Jr, 'Ignorance, System and Sacrifice: A Literary Reading of the *Prioress's Tale*', *Poetica* 15/16 (1983), 136–53 (at p. 138).

response to the clergeon 'lacks mature detachment, 'that she enters too completely into the child's world, indeed that she identifies with him'.[50] But the manner in which she relates how Mary is moved by the note of uncorrupted sanctity which inspires the clergeon to learn the *Alma redemptoris Mater* 'al by rote', even though 'nought wiste he what this Latyn was to seye',[51] seems to establish an artful, implicit parallel between his *sanctitas*, which is grounded in *humilitas*,[52] and her own, divinely authorised, song of praise. However, this song is presented as a seemingly artless *symbolon* of faith, which mirrors the clergeon's humble profession in its *sancta simplicitas*. The fact that he is 'seven yeer of age', the first climacteric when the age of innocence is superseded by that of 'the whining schoolboy, with his satchel / And shining morning face, creeping like snail unwillingly to school',[53] serves to heighten the pathos of his martyrdom in the octave of martyrs, Stephen Protomartyr (December 26th), John the Evangelist (December 27th), the Holy Innocents (December 28th in the Latin Church), and St Thomas of Canterbury (December 29th).[54] Thus there is an ironic poignance to his aspiration to 'konne it al er Cristemasse be went',[55] as, like the *sancti innocentes* before him, he will be gathered to God before the season is out. However, this homely, affective *Andachtsbild* of the little martyr-to-be, unwittingly doing what 'smale children doon in hire childhede',[56] is framed by an unfamiliar, orientalised backdrop, which is dominated by the *perfida plebs* of the Old Dispensation, now classed among the enemies of God.

It has been stated repeatedly that the Asiatic setting serves to distance both Chaucer and the Prioress from the 'incidental anti-Semitism' of the *Tale*.[57] Zitter sums this viewpoint: it 'takes place long

---

[50] Friedman, 'Chaucer's Anti-Semitism', pp. 124–5.

[51] *Prioress's Tale*, ll. 522–3, *Riverside Chaucer*, p. 210.

[52] Matthew 18. 3. Cf. also Hawkins, 'Chaucer's Prioress', p. 602, n. 9, who notes in relation to Matthew 2: 16 that the 'association of infancy and humility (as in Psalm 130) became a medieval commonplace'.

[53] *As You Like It*, II. 7. 145–7. Cf. Hawkins, 'Chaucer's Prioress', pp. 607–8.

[54] See L. Ruth, '*Salvete Flores Martyrum*: The Feast of the Innocent Infants in the Early Church', *Ecclesia Orans* 12 (1995), 373–93, esp. pp. 380–6. On the Mass of St Thomas in the Sarum Use, see J. C. Wenk, 'On the Sources of *The Prioress's Tale*', *Mediaeval Studies* 17 (1955), 214–19 (at pp. 217–18).

[55] *Prioress's Tale*, ll. 540, *Riverside Chaucer*, p. 210.

[56] Ibid., 501.

[57] Hardy Long Frank, 'Chaucer's Prioress and the Blessed Virgin', *Chaucer Review* 13 (1978), 346–62 (at p. 358).

ago and far away in a great city in Asia',[58] and is thus set at a remove from the contemporary context. However, the *locus* is more than simply a historico-topographical pretext, as it is representative of a trend discernible in the visual arts, which comes to fruition after the final expulsion of the Jews from France in 1394.[59] While there was a well-established tradition of caricaturing Jews, which extended at least as far back as the First Crusade, they were generally depicted as members of contemporary society, albeit an outgroup identifiably different in appearance and dress, with evidence of the influence of discriminatory laws from the thirteenth century onwards.[60] However, as Jews increasingly become exotic figures of folktale in the fourteenth and fifteenth centuries, there is a tendency to depict them in an ahistorical and distinctly Asiatic context.[61] They are no longer depicted as readily identifiable outsiders in contemporary society,[62] but rather as beyond the farthest palisades of that society; a paradigm of Otherness suspended in an orientalised timelessness. Thus, in *The Prioress's Tale* the *locus* not only reflects the contemporary and ecclesiologically tractable recrudescence the association of Jews with Saracens, but also the sense of timelessness conveyed by the fact that

[58] E. Stark Zitter, 'Anti-Semitism in Chaucer's *Prioress's Tale*', *Chaucer Review* 25 (1990–1), 277–84 (at p. 287).

[59] See in particular S. Menache, 'The King, the Church and the Jews: Some Considerations on the Expulsions from England and France', *Journal of Medieval History* 13 (1987), 223–36; R. Kohn, *Les Juifs de la France du Nord dans la seconde moitié du XIVe siècle*, Collection de la Revue des Etudes Juives (Louvain, 1988); W. C. Jordan, *The French Monarchy and the Jews: From Philip Augustus to the Last Capetians* (Philadelphia: Institut des Etudes Augustiniennes, 1989); N. Coulet, 'L'expulsion des Juifs de France', *L'histoire* 139 (1990), 8–16.

[60] See B. Blumenkranz, *Le Juif médiéval au mirroir de l'art chrétien* (Paris, 1966), esp. pp. 19–35.

[61] 'L'expulsion «définitive» des Juifs de France intervient en 1394. Dès 1410, quand a été peinte par les frères de Limbourg une partie de la Bible historiée qui semble avoir été destinée à Jean de Berry, nous rencontrons dans la représentation des Juifs un mélange curieux de connaissance authentique et de fantaisie artistique. Malgré les papillotes et la barbe fournie, l'homme à droite, avec son phylactère en blanc, donne plutôt l'impression d'un Oriental que d'un Juif, avec son couvre-chef en forme de turban. Cette «orientalisation» des Juifs dans la représentation artistique se rencontre couramment en France, au xve siècle, où l'on ne connaît plus de Juifs sur place' (ibid., p. 36).

[62] Cf. S. Menache, 'Faith, Myth and Politics: The Stereotype of the Jews and their Expulsion from England and France', *Jewish Quarterly Review*, ns. 75 (1985), 351–74.

nothing ever changes, 'yeer by yere',[63] which facilitates the use of scriptural telescoping in an apparently secular context.

But there are elements in the depiction of this Asiatic Jewry that are reminiscent of the vestigial traces of Jewish life in Western Europe, particularly France and England. Alexander notes that the 'realistic topographical detail' seems to suggest that Chaucer 'was directly acquainted with Jewish ghettoes'.[64] However that might be, in the context presented here, a 'strete' which is 'free and open at eyther ende', it is important to note Stacey's analysis of the close contact between Jew and Christian before the expulsion in 1290:

> There were no Jewish ghettos in medieval England. Jews and Christians lived cheek by jowl with each other. One could point to certain neighborhoods in a town as constituting 'the Jewry', but this description reflected only the relatively higher density of Jewish settlement in those areas. Christian churches occupied prominent places in the streets of the Jewry – increasingly prominent places in some towns, as thirteenth-century kings began to confiscate Jewish synagogues and turn them into churches. And Christian neighbors would always be close at hand. One *schola Judaeorum* in London actually shared a wall with the church of the penitential friars, until the king ordered the yeshiva pulled down, because of the 'continuous caterwauling' of the Jews was a distraction to the friars' divine service. This was an atmosphere which pressed toward extremes of behaviour.[65]

A localised sense of living 'cheek by jowl' with the Jews, which is designed to dredge up memories of the not too distant past, punctuates the Prioress's atemporal narrative. We may note in particular the fact that the 'litel scole of Cristen folk ther stod / Doun at the ferther ende' of the Jewry;[66] the Jews are 'sustained by a lord of that contree / For foule usure and lucre of vileynye',[67] and on hearing the daily intonation

[63] *Prioress's Tale*, ll. 498, *Riverside Chaucer*, p. 210.
[64] 'Madam Eglentyne', p. 118; *Prioress's Tale*, ll. 493–4, *Riverside Chaucer*, p. 209. See also R. Adams, 'Chaucer's "New Rachael" and the Theological Roots of Medieval Anti-Semitism', *Bulletin of the John Rylands Library* 77 (1995), 9–18 (at p. 10).
[65] R. C. Stacey, 'The Conversion of Jews to Christianity in Thirteenth-Century England', *Speculum* 67 (1992), 263–83 (at pp. 264–5), who points out that St Mary's in Jewry, London, is one such church. We may also note the example of All Saints Jewry, Cambridge.
[66] *Prioress's Tale*, ll. 498, *Riverside Chaucer*, p. 210.
[67] *Prioress's Tale*, ll. 490–1, *Riverside Chaucer*, p. 209. Cf. Alexander, 'Madam

of a Marian hymn down their 'strete', they characteristically resort to *ira mala*.[68] There is also, of course, the very localised reference to the murder of 'young Hugh of Lyncoln';[69] thus the murder of the clergeon in the Asiatic Jewry is not only associated with the most notorious instance of the Ritual Murder Myth in English history,[70] but also with a grisly, folk martyrology of little boys 'ycomen of Cristen blood'.

Although the Ritual Murder myth 'originated purely as vilification, it was yet calculated to assume the proportions of actuality in the mind of the uncritical'.[71] The first recorded case of Ritual Murder persecu-

Eglentyne', pp. 114–15: 'The charge is incidental to the main thrust of the story and plays no direct part in the development of the plot, but it is more than local colour. Dramatically it helps to justify the gory punishment meted out to the Jews at the end.' See also A. Kirschenbaum, 'Jewish and Christian Theories of Usury in the Middle Ages', *Jewish Quarterly Review* 75 (1985), 270–89; J. Shatzmiller, *Shylock Reconsidered: Jews, Moneylending and Medieval Society* (Berkeley, 1990); Y. Barzel, 'Confiscation by the Ruler: The Rise and Fall of Jewish Lending in the Middle Ages', *Journal of Law and Economics* 35 (1992), 1–14.

[68] The ultimate manifestation of *mala ira* is homicide; cf. J. Cohen, 'The Jews as the Killers of Christ in the Latin Tradition, from Augustine to the Friars', *Traditio* 39 (1983), 1–27, esp. p. 6–8; S. Rohrbacher, 'The Charge of Deicide: An Anti-Jewish Motif in Medieval Christian Art', *Journal of Medieval History* 17 (1991), 292–322. However, in *The Parson's Tale*, the Jews are particularly associated with blasphemy; cf. X. 593–600, *Riverside Chaucer*, p. 307. In the context of the typographical significance of the clergeon's daily route, it is interesting to note an incident that occurred on Ascension Day 1268, when 'an Oxford Jew violently attacked an ecclesiastical procession marching down St Aldates (the heart of Oxford's Jewry), trampling on the processional cross and spitting on it.' In the aftermath, the Jewish community were forced to pay for a stone cross 'to be permanently fixed facing directly into the Jewry, with a description of the outrage which had prompted its construction prominently engraved upon it' (Stacey, 'Conversion of Jews', p. 265). Cf. C. Cluse, 'Stories of Breaking and Taking the Cross: A Possible Context for the Oxford Incident of 1268', *Revue d'Histoire Ecclésiastique* 90 (1995), 396–442.

[69] *Prioress's Tale*, II. 684, *Riverside Chaucer*, p. 212.

[70] See G. I. Langmuir, 'The Knight's Tale of Young Hugh of Lincoln', *Speculum* 47 (1972), 459–82; S. Ferris, 'Chaucer at Lincoln (1387): The *Prioress's Tale* as a Political Poem', *Chaucer Review* 15 (1981), 295–321.

[71] Trachtenberg, *Devil and the Jews*, p. 21. Cf. C. Ocker, 'Ritual Murder and the Subjectivity of Christ: A Choice in Medieval Christianity', *Harvard Theological Review* 91 (1998), 153–92 (at p. 154, n. 3): 'Ritual murder is the belief that Jews kill Christians for ritual purposes. Blood libel is the allegation that, in so doing, Jews extract blood for their rites or for magic.' See also Trachtenberg, *Devil and the Jews*, pp. 124–55; M. Simon, 'Christian Anti-Semitism', in *Essential Papers on Judaism and Christianity in Conflict* ed. J. Cohen (New York: New York University Press, 1991), pp. 131–73; R. Erb, 'Zur Erforschung der europäischen

tion is thought to be the alleged martyrdom of the English boy William of Norwich, a twelve-year-old skinner's apprentice, found dead during Easter, 1144.[72] At least four other accusations of Ritual Murder occurred in England during the twelfth century, most notably in Gloucester in 1168. Here, local Jews and some from other communities who had come together to celebrate a *bris* were accused of the torture and subsequent crucifixion of little Harold, 'whose body was found in the Severn after he had been missing for twenty-two days'.[73] Little Robert of Bury St Edmunds was reputed to have been murdered in secret by a Jew in 1181; a Bristol boy called Adam was supposedly martyred around 1183,[74] and the Winchester Jewry were accused of ritually sacrificing a French boy during the Passover season of 1192.[75]

There are over twenty cases of alleged Ritual Murder recorded throughout Western Europe during the thirteenth century, and the

Ritualmordbeschuldigungen', in *Die Legende vom Ritualmord: Zur Geschichte der Blutbeschuldigungen gegen Juden*, Dokumente, Texte, Materialen 6 ed. R. Erb (Berlin, 1993), pp. 9–16.

[72] A. Jessop and M. R. James, *St William of Norwich* (Cambridge, 1896); V. D. Lipman, *The Jews of Medieval Norwich* (London, 1967), esp. pp. 3–18; G. I. Langmuir, 'Thomas of Monmouth: Detector of Ritual Murder', *Speculum* 59 (1984), 820–46; *idem*, 'Historiographic Crucifixion', in *Les Juifs en regard de l'histoire: mélanges en l'honneur de Bernhard Blumenkranz* (Paris: Picard, 1985), pp. 109–27; F. Lotter, 'Innocens virgo et martyr: Thomas von Monmouth und die Verbreitung der Ritualmordlegende im Hochmittelalter', in *Die Legende vom Ritualmord*, pp. 25–72; J. M. McCulloh, 'Jewish Ritual Murder: William of Norwich, Thomas of Monmouth, and the Early Dissemination of the Myth', *Speculum* 72 (1997), 698–740. Cf. also the English summary of I. J. Yuval, 'Vengeance and Damnation, Blood and Defamation: From Jewish Martyrdom to Blood Libel Accusations', *Zion* 58 (1993), 33–90, at pp. vi-viii, who challenges Langmuir's assertion that the case of William of Norwich was the first instance of the allegation, sourcing it in the aftermath of the Rhenish pogroms of 1096.

[73] Langmuir, 'Knight's Tale', p. 462. Cf. J. Hillaby, 'The Ritual Child-Murder Accusation: Its Dissemination and Harold of Gloucester', *Jewish Historical Studies* 34 (1994–6), 69–109.

[74] C. Cluse, '"Fabula ineptissiam". Die Ritualmordlegende um Adam von Bristol nach der Handschrift London, British Library, Harley 957', *Aschkenas* 5 (1995), 293–330.

[75] *The Chronicle of Richard of Devizes of the Time of King Richard the First*, ed. J. T. Appleby (London: Nelson, 1963), p. 68, refers to the 'seua suauitas et blesa benignitas' of the Winchester Jewry. See also P. Allin, 'Richard of Devizes and the Alleged Martyrdom of a Boy at Winchester', *Transactions of the Jewish Historical Society of England* 27 (1978–80), 32–9; G. Mentgen, 'Richard of Devizes und die Juden: Ein Beitrag zur Interpretation seiner "Gesta Richardi"', *Kairos* 30–1 (1988–9), 95–104; A. Bale, 'Richard of Devizes and Fictions of Judaism', *Jewish Culture and History* 3 (2000), 55–72.

Blood Libel makes its appearance around 1235.[76] According to Po-Chia Hsia, 'The number of accusations multiplied threefold during the thirteenth century', but 'dropped slightly in the fourteenth'. Indeed, instances where the Blood Libel and the Ritual Murder Myth are invoked are not recorded in Western Europe after the fourteenth century, and this is linked to the expulsion of the Jews from England and France,[77] but it is important to remember that such pernicious accusations are still current during Chaucer's lifetime. Thus, although the Prioress states that the alleged martyrdom of Hugh of Lincoln occurred 'but a litel while ago',[78] when it actually took place in 1255, the fact that these accusations are still prevalent, continuing to spread 'eastward like an epidemic from England and France',[79] lends a heightened sense of immediacy to his sacrificial testimony, and that of all the little local lads before him.

Thus even if we readily acknowledge that there is no suggestion of the Ritual Murder Myth in the *Tale* itself,[80] there is a skilful, polyvalent parallelism established between the clergeon, the evocation of the local crop of boy martyrs in the reference to little Saint Hugh, 'crucified in repetition and mockery of the death of Christ',[81] and Christ himself, because all are murdered by the perfidious, satanic Jews whose victims' blood cry out for *ultio sanguinis*.[82] Moreover, this parallelism reaches its apogee in the abject image of the clergeon, with his slit throat, mired in a privy 'where as thise Jewes purgen hire entraille',[83] who summarily

---

[76] H. L. Strack, *The Jew and Human Sacrifice*, trans. H. Blanchamp, 8th ed. (London, 1909); C. Roth, 'The Feast of Purim and the Origins of the Blood Accusation', *Speculum* 8 (1933), 520–6; A. Dundes, 'The Ritual Murder or Blood Libel Legend: A Study of Anti-Semitic Victimization through Projective Inversion', in *The Blood Libel Legend: A Case-Book in Anti-Semitic Folklore*, ed. A. Dundes (Madison, Wis.: University of Wisconsin Press, 1991), pp. 336–76.

[77] R. Po-Chia Hsia, *The Myth of Ritual Murder: Jews and Magic in Reformation Germany* (New Haven and London: Yale University Press, 1988), p. 3.

[78] *Prioress's Tale*, ll. 686, *Riverside Chaucer*, p. 212.

[79] Hsia, *The Myth of Ritual Murder*, p. 3.

[80] Cf. Friedman, 'Chaucer's Anti-Semitism', pp. 118–19; Alexander, 'Madame Eglentyne', p. 113.

[81] Alexander, 'Madame Eglentyne', p. 113.

[82] Psalm 78. 10; cf. Genesis 4. 10. See also *Prioress's Tale*, II, 576–7, *Riverside Chaucer*, p. 211: 'And namely ther th'onour of God shall sprede; / The blood out crieth on youre cursed dede.'

[83] Ibid., 573. Cf. Langmuir, 'Knight's Tale', p. 461: 'little Hugh, the eight-year old son of a widow, Beatrice, accidentally fell into a cesspool attached to a Jew's house'. It is worth noting that this detail is echoed in the cloacal atmosphere of the tale of Abraham of Berkhamsted, yet another tale of Jewish blasphemy and

overleaps his lacerated prisonhouse of flesh to join the 144,000 in Revelation 14. 4, 'who were not defiled with women: for they were virgins'. As Nolan observes, 'There is no more remarkable, bizarre juxtaposition of bodily degradation and spiritual purity in the whole of the *Canterbury Tales* than this.'[84] Now the clergeon stands 'Biforn this Lamb and synge a song al newe, / That nevere, flesshly, wommen they ne knewe';[85] he participates in 'the great multitude' of Revelation 7. 9–10, standing 'in sight of the Lamb, clothed with white robes, and palms in their hands', singing the sonorous and mighty song of praise that only the 144,000 can learn.[86] Although the Holy Virgins were often directly identified as the Holy Innocents, the *flores martyrum*,[87] they were also interpreted as inclusive of the total harvest of first fruits gathered to God and to the Lamb *sine macula*, such as this 'gemme of chastite'.[88]

In keeping with the proleptic intertextuality of prefiguration in type and fulfilment in antitype, the clergeon is not only portrayed as one of the Holy Virgins, but like the Holy Innocents, he is a *figura* of Christ, the Man of Sorrows who was led to slaughter like a lamb,[89] despised and rejected by the impious as 'weak, detestable, wretched, a man condemned to a most shameful death'.[90] Similarly, his mother is not only portrayed as a *figura* of Mary as *Mater Dolorosa*, who receives the broken body of her Son in her arms and weeps, but also as the 'newe Rachel'.[91] This echoes the supersessionist exegesis, grounded in Matthew 2. 17–18, whereby the lamentation of the disconsolate matriarch in Ramah for the children of Israel is fulfilled and renewed in the lamentation of the bereaved mothers in Bethlehem for the

homicide from the corrosive pen of Matthew of Paris; cf. ibid., p. 463. On this point see also Cluse, ' "Fabula ineptissima" ', p. 308; Bale, 'Richard of Devizes', p. 60,

[84] 'Chaucer's Tales of Transcendence', p. 36.

[85] *Prioress's Tale*, ll. 584–5, *Riverside Chaucer*, p. 211.

[86] Cf. Revelation 2. 17; 19. 12.

[87] The epithet would seem to originate in 'Quicumque Christum quaeritis', of the *Cathemerinon* of Prudentius; cf. *Prudentius*, trans. H. J. Thomson, Loeb, 2 vols (London and Cambridge, Mass., 1949–53), I, 110, line 125: 'salvete, flores martyrum'.

[88] *Prioress's Tale*, ll. 584–5, *Riverside Chaucer*, p. 211. Cf. Deuteronomy 26. 2; Revelation 14. 5.

[89] Isaiah 53. 7.

[90] Bernard of Clairvaux, 'Sermon 28', *On the Song of Songs II*, trans. K. Walsh, intr. J. Leclercq (Kalamazoo, MI: Medieval Institute Publications, 1976), p. 91, paraphrasing Wisdom of Solomon 2. 20.

[91] *Prioress's Tale*, l. 627, *Riverside Chaucer*, p. 211.

children of the New Covenant, slaughtered by Herod.[92] As the Bethlehemite mother is not only a type of Mary cradling her Crucified son, but also of Mary cradling her suckling infant, the Mother of God is revealed by association as the antitype of Rachael, who is the true Church, in whom faith subsisted when the apostles fled.[93] Thus it is interesting to speculate if the contemporary ecclesiological debates as to whether the true Church may at times only 'subsist in the soul of a single individual', as it did in Mary's after Christ's death, and the related argument 'which also included the possibility that faith may remain in a small group only',[94] such as a Christian minority in an orientalised setting, inform the contrast drawn by the Prioress between the attendant abbot 'that was a holy man', and those who 'oghte be';[95] an apt comment on the problems bedevilling the institutionalised Church, a body almost severed from its cloven head by schism,[96] but from within.

[92] 'Then was fulfilled that which was spoken by Jeremias the prophet, saying: 'A voice in Rama was heard, lamentation and great mourning; Rachel bewailing her children, and would not be comforted, because they are not.' Cf. Jeremiah 31. 14. See in particular M. W. Bloomfield, 'Chaucer's Sense of History', *Journal of English and Germanic Philology* 51 (1952), 301–13 (at p. 98); Zitter, 'Anti-Semitism', p. 279; Adams, 'Chaucer's "New Rachael"', pp. 14–17, esp. 18, who summarises 'the claim that Christianity has inherited and co-opted the Covenant, that the Church is the new Israel (or Rachael, for that matter), and that all of the Old Testament can properly be interpreted only in light of this axiom'.

[93] For a particularly rich iconological analysis of the Ramah-Bethlehem-Golgotha typology see R. Binion, 'Three Mourning Mothers: The Making and Unmaking of a Christian Figural Complex', *Journal of Psychohistory* 26 (1998), 449–77, esp. p. 458: 'the several extant versions of the *Ordo Rachelis*, a liturgical drama of the eleventh and twelfth centuries that was performed on Innocents Day or Epiphany, featured a Rachael fantastically spirited to Bethlehem to mourn the slain Innocents and repeatedly termed this Rachael in Bethlehem a sorrowing virgin mother, thereby identifying that sorrowing nonvirgin mother in so many words with the sorrowing virgin mother at the cross'. Cf. K. Young, 'Ordo Rachelis', in *University of Wisconsin Studies in Language and Literature* 4 (1919), pp. 1–65, esp. 18, 30, 33, 35, 47.

[94] Denny, 'Avignon Pietà', pp. 214–15; cf. Congar, 'Incidence ecclésiologique', p. 287, n. 2, who cites Pierre d'Ailly, *Utrum Petri ecclesia lege reguletur*, in J. Gerson, *Opera Omnia*, ed. L. Ellies Du Pin, 5 vols (Antwerp, 1706), I, 671. See F. Oakley, *The Political Thought of Pierre d'Ailly: The Voluntarist Tradition* (New Haven, 1964); esp. pp. 148–9; 152–4; B. Guenée, *Between Church and State: The Lives of Four French Prelates in the Late Middle Ages*, trans. A. Goldhammer (Chicago and London: University of Chicago Press, 1991), pp. 102–258.

[95] *Prioress's Tale*, ll. 642–3, *Riverside Chaucer*, p. 211.

[96] On the Church as *soma Christou*, cf. I Corinthians 12. 12, 27; 6. 15;

Furthermore, the eidetic image of the clergeon's mother 'swownynge by his beere' (line 625),[97] not only recalls a variation of the iconographic motif of the Bethlehemite mother in which she grieves 'over a tiny son stretched out dead before her',[98] but also the emergent iconographic motif of the *Pietà*, in which 'culminated the transcendent triunity of the lamenting mother in Bethlehem with both Rachel before her and Mary after her'.[99]

However, the shadow cast by this lambent transcendence is that the Children of Israel, who 'are not',[100] as least as far as Chaucer's England is concerned, and over whom Rachael wept, become 'the cursed folk of Herode al newe'.[101] Thus the anti-Judaic predella that forms an appendage to the tender scene of the mother's *spasimo* is a fitting artefact for the 'special period of judicial cruelty'.[102] The Prioress's flinty appropriation of Old Covenant law, 'Yvele shal have that yvele wol deserve',[103] is in keeping with the suppersessionist logic of *adversus Judaeos* polemic,[104] and complements the gratuitous nature of the sentence meted out by the provost,[105] he a grimly condign antitype of the type of Pagan Magistrate familiar from patristic hagiographic narratives. It is also a mighty act of self-assertion which renders the subtleties of 'doctrine as men used'[106] a thing indifferent when faced with the enemies of God; it represents 'the triumph of the unschooled,

Ephesians 4. 4, 16, 25; 5. 30; Colossians 2. 19. See also H. de Lubac, *Corpus Mysticum: L'Eucharistie et l'église au Moyen Age* (Paris: Aubier, 1944), pp. 117–37; E. H. Kantorowicz, *The King's Two Bodies: A Study in Mediaeval Political Theology* (Princeton: Princeton University Press, 1957), pp. 194–206, esp. 195.

[97] *Prioress's Tale*, ll. 625, *Riverside Chaucer*, p. 211.

[98] Binion, 'Three Mourning Mothers', p. 455. See also A. Hiemann, 'The Capital Frieze and Pilasters of the Portail Royal, Chartres', *Journal of the Warburg and Courtauld Institutes* 31 (1968), 73–102 (at p. 80); W. Sauerländer, *Gothic Sculpture in France 1140–1270* (London: Thames and Hudson, 1972), pp. 386, 388–91, 394.

[99] Binion, 'Three Mourning Mothers', p. 464.

[100] Jeremiah 31. 15.

[101] *Prioress's Tale*, ll. 574, *Riverside Chaucer*, p. 210.

[102] J. Huizinga, *The Waning of the Middle Ages: A Study of the Forms of Life, Thought, and Art in France and the Netherlands in the Fourteenth and Fifteenth Centuries*, trans. F. Hopman (London: Arnold, 1924, repr. London, 1990), p. 22.

[103] *Prioress's Tale*, ll. 632, *Riverside Chaucer*, p. 211.

[104] On this point see Ocker, 'Ritual Murder', pp. 88–9.

[105] *Prioress's Tale*, ll. 633–4, *Riverside Chaucer*, p. 211. Cf. R. Rex, 'Wild Horses, Justice and Charity in the Prioress's Tale', *Papers on Language and Literature* 22 (1986), 339–51.

[106] *Prioress's Tale*, ll. 499, *Riverside Chaucer*, p. 210.

pietistic voice and the punishment awaiting those who deny the authority of this voice'.[107] During Chaucer's lifetime, the subversive, coercive strength of such a voice is clearly illustrated by the case of Catherine of Siena, stigmatic, anorexic and somewhat atypical Doctor of the Church. As a humble Dominican lay sister, described by her confessor and biographer, Raymond of Capua, as *laica et illiterata*, she displayed no fear in preaching to Pope Gregory XI, even threatening the supreme ruler of the Church on earth with a higher force, if he did not pay heed to her divinely inspired directives: 'See to it that I do not complain about you to the crucified Christ.'[108] By invoking the transcendent power of Christ and his Holy Mother, marginalised figures in society, particularly women, who were in their daily lives denied political, ecclesiastical and intellectual roles, could lay claim to an authority otherwise prohibited to them. Similarly, we may note that the Prioress exults in the cautionary aspect of her *Tale*, which not only bears witness to the paradoxical strength of the transfixed Virgin to pierce the heart of all but the hard-hearted Jews,[109] but also serves as a divinely inspired commination to blasphemous heretics and doubting Thomases, or smart Alecs or Geoffreys for that matter. In this context, it is significant that the narrative relies on hagiographic facts, the 'facts of fantasy',[110] which transcend the reality defined and governed by politicians, ecclesiastics and intellectuals. Indeed, her unregenerate sense of the numinous has the desired effect on even the 'men of dignitee' in her audience: 'Whan seyd was al this miracle, every man / As sobre was that wonder was to se'.[111] Thus the Prioress confounds any potential enemies of God enfolded in the riven cloak of *Mater Ecclesia*, but as far as the bloodied confutation of Ecclesia's typological predecessor is concerned, the rest is lamentably not silence.

---

[107] Robertson, 'Aspects of Female Piety', p. 154.
[108] St Catherine of Siena, Letter 255, *Epistolario I* (Rome, 1966), p. 93, quoted in translation by C. Leonardi, 'Intellectuals and Hagiography in the Fourteenth Century', in *Intellectuals and Writers in Fourteenth-Century Europe: The J. A. W. Bennett Memorial Lectures, Perugia 1984*, ed. P. Boitani and A. Torti (Cambridge: Cambridge University Press, 1986), pp. 7–19 (at p. 31).
[109] See Matthew 19. 8; Ezekiel 3. 7, and Ezekiel 9. 9; Zechariah 7. 12. Cf. *Prioress's Tale*, ll. 555–6, *Riverside Chaucer*, p. 210.
[110] Leonardi, 'Intellectuals and Hagiography', p. 9.
[111] *Prioress's Tale*, ll. 555–6, *Riverside Chaucer*, p. 210.

Notes on Contributors

Anne Marie D'Arcy   is Lecturer in Medieval Literature in the Department of English at the University of Leicester. Her research concentrates on medieval and Renaissance Wisdom Literature, Iconology and the patristic sources of Old and Middle English Literature. Her most recent publication is *Wisdom and the Grail: The Image of the Vessel in 'Queste del Saint Graal' and Malory's 'Tale of the Sankgreal'* (2000).

Hugh Magennis   is Professor of Old English Literature in the School of English, Queen's University Belfast. He is the author of numerous articles and books, including *Anglo-Saxon Appetites: Food and Drink and Their Consumption in Old English and Related Literature* (1999), and *The Old English Life of St Mary of Egypt* (2002). He is currently working on Old English prose saints' lives and on aspects of the language of Old English poetry.

David Salter   is a Lecturer in Medieval Literature in the Department of English at the University of Edinburgh. His most recent publication is *Holy and Noble Beasts: Encounters with Animals in Medieval Literature* (2001). He is currently working on representations of St Francis and the Franciscan Movement in medieval literature.

Mary Swan   is Director of Studies at the Centre for Medieval Studies, University of Leeds. She is currently researching the transmission of Old English texts in the post-Conquest period, and women in Old English prose. She is a founder of the Research Group on Post-Conquest Old English Manuscripts, and the co-editor of *Rewriting Old English in the Twelfth Century* (with Elaine Treharne, 2000). She has also published numerous articles on the dissemination and adaptation of homiletic and hagiographic texts in the eleventh and twelfth centuries.

Elaine Treharne   is Professor of Medieval Literature in the Department of English at the University of Leicester. She is Chair of the English Association, and Second Vice President of the International Society of Anglo-Saxonists. Her research interests are primarily in the field of manuscript studies (c. 1000–1200). Her publications include *Old and Middle English: An Anthology* (2000), and *A Companion to Anglo-Saxon Literature* (with Phillip Pulsiano, 2001).

Greg Walker   is Professor of Early-Modern Literature and Culture in the Department of English at the University of Leicester. He currently holds a Leverhulme Major Research Fellowship. He has published widely on medieval drama and early modern literature. His most recent publications include *Medieval Drama: An Anthology* (2000) and *Writing Under Tyranny: English Literature and the Henrician Reformation* (forthcoming).

Index